THE BIG BOOK OF
Yorkshire Wit & Wisdom

Dalesman

First published in Great Britain in 2013 by Dalesman Publishing
an imprint of
Country Publications Ltd
The Water Mill, Broughton Hall
Skipton, North Yorkshire BD23 3AG

ISBN 978-1-85568-315-0

Printed in China by 1010 Printing.

Introduction

When the *Yorkshire Dalesman* was first published in April 1939 it had a modest office in Clapham. It cost three old pence and it is a miracle that it is still thriving to this day. The magazine, with its wartime paper restrictions, could well have ceased to publish but such was its popularity that the title was produced on time every month and continued to attract the most distinguished authors to be found in the county.

During the compiling of this book I have been fortunate enough to trawl through the *Dalesman* archives, and I realised just how little the humour has changed over the years.

A German friend of mine told me he loves Yorkshire because "the folk there are happy to laugh and poke fun at each other. I always look forward to reading my copy of *Dalesman*, which always puts a smile on my face". This is the beauty of 'tyke talk' — it puts a smile on all our faces.

It is right to entitle this a 'Big Book' because it has to encompass a county full to the brim with wit, wisdom and humour.

Ron Freethy

A MAN who wrote and asked whether a hotel in Settle permitted dogs had the following reply:

"I've been in the hotel business for over thirty years. Never yet have I had to call the police to eject a disorderly dog in the wee small hours of the morning. No dog has ever passed a dud cheque on me. Never yet has a dog set the bedclothes alight from smoking in bed. No dog has ever failed to pay his bar bill. I've never found a hotel blanket or cutlery in a dog's suitcase. Your dog's welcome.

PS. If the dog will vouch for you, then you can come as well."

A SMALL boy at a Scarborough school was asked the difference between prose and poetry. He pondered for a while and then said:

"'There was a young man named Rees, who went into the sea up to his ankles' — that's prose; but if the water had a been a few inches higher it would have been poetry."

A Dewsbury market stallholder was the victim of petty thieving. He wrote on a notice which he displayed on his stall:

"The Lord helps them who help themselves, but the Lord help those caught helping themselves here."

A FARM lad in the Wolds was driving ducks from the village pond when a large car arrived in the village. The driver — an 'out of towner' — cast an approving eye over the fine, fat birds, and with the idea of purchasing one for himself he stopped the car and hailed the farm lad.

"Hey, you," he called out, "How often do you kill your ducks?"

The lad stared at him for a minute, thinking things out and marvelling at the questions asked by chaps out of town, before replying:

"Why, mister, nobbut once."

A three-year-old boy, who was accustomed to listening to the shipping forecast on the radio, said to his screaming new baby sister:

"What's the matter, luvvie, you got a depression?"

MARY WAS a keen rambler in the North York Moors, and on her outings she would often stop at village pubs for various refreshments. She kept a little diary in which she jotted down brief descriptions of her walks and the names of all the places she visited, and one day Mary showed the diary to a friend who had called round to see her. The friend was intrigued, and somewhat

"We need cars to get away from the pollution caused by cars."

puzzled, about the initials 'R-C' written in red ink against the names of certain pubs.

"There seems to be quite a lot of owners of pubs who are Roman Catholics," she commented.

"Oh no," Mary replied, "those are the ones where I got rum in the coffee."

THE SUBJECT of garden rivalry prompts the story over-heard at the auction mart of a local man who was bragging of his potato crop. He had never before had so big a yield and they were all so large.

"There wun't a pig-tatie among 'em," he declared, "and mi wife couldn't get more ner two on 'em into 'er biggest pan — and those two fed all t' family."

"IN SOME areas, public houses had a bar called the four-ale bar. I have read somewhere that they got their name from selling four-penny ale. This may be true but I am inclined to believe that such bars got their name from selling the full range of ales — usually four. I remember some of the best Tennant's pubs proudly displayed four pump handles on the bar — Best Bitter, Ordinary Bitter, Rock Ale (mild) and Queen's Ale, a premium beer. Although it is probably forty years since Queen's Ale was last brewed, I can still remember it as the best beer that I have ever tasted — and that is saying quite a lot."

Frank Priestley

Overheard on a coach tour through the Dales:

"That's the oldest inn there."

"The oldest in where?"

"The oldest inn there."

"What — here or there?"

"Gosh, let's get out and have a drink."

A LIBRARIAN caught site of a small boy with a book, *Advice for young Mothers*. She asked him why he wanted to borrow this title and he replied:

"I collect moths for nature study. It is what I've been wanting for a long time. Have you anything better?"

"Are you t' town rat-catcher?"

A VISITOR walking down a village street in Aysgarth one summer's night heard the singing of the local choir. He stopped to listen. One of the locals was standing by admiring the sweet chirrup of the cricket.

"What beautiful singing," commented the stranger.

"Aye," replied the dalesman, "they do it by rubbing their hind legs together."

A LAZY miner was sitting by the fire when he said to his wife:

"Eye, lass, will ter put cat out?"

"Why?" asked his wife.

"Cos it's a-fire," he growled.

A hot coal had fallen on it and set fire to its tail.

Spanish watter

If ivver yer goa on a picnic
Yer allus tak' summat to sup;
It might be just pop, milk or watter,
Or tea in a flask wi' a cup.

But Ah think 'at t' best's Spanish Watter,
It's cheap an' it's easy to mak'.
It costs a few coppers for t' spanish,
But then all it wants is a shak'.

If yer mek it reet strong when yer startin'
Then sup it about halfway dahn,
Yer can fill up ter t' top wi' cowd watter
To last yer where ivver yer gahn.

Ah must ha supped gallons o' picnics,
An' made it last all t' time Ah'm aht;
Ah've wattered it dahn when it lowered
Till my Spanish Watter wor baht!

Will Clemence

A WHOLE page would be needed to catalogue the varied products of William Beck, the Scosthrop joiner. He had on hand a garage, a ferret box, a replica of an antique cupboard and several rakes, whilst a gate, which he had just completed, stood in the yard.

He uses an oil engine to drive his circular saw and lathe, but he has not neglected the traditional hand method, and the auger, adze, and moulding planes are brightly polished with recent use.

Local timber is still largely employed and formerly this was all cut by hand. A frame pit-saw hangs on the wall as a reminder of those days but the saw-pit has long been filled in. The saw blade, about five feet long, was strengthened by stout wooden framework to which handles were attached at each end. The timber was arranged lengthways along the pit, and two men, a top sawyer who directed the sawing operations, and a bottom sawyer, who had all the hard work and sawdust, operated the saw to cut the tree into planks.

The country joiner is essentially concerned with the manufacture of rural products such as ladders, sheep-stocks, hayrakes, gates, malls, swingle trees and milking stools, but he must be equally prepared to turn wringing-machine rollers, to make carts and to carry out general household repairs.

The Scosthorp joiner, like many another village joiner, is a coffin maker too, and he has made the 'last suits', as he calls his coffins, for many of his old village acquaintances.

AN AIREDALE millworker, who was a heavy pipe smoker, had with great daring tried a packet of herb tobacco to mix with his normal supply. The experiment was watched intently by his eleven-year-old son, who suddenly asked him:

"Have you ever tried coltsfoot, daddy?"

"No," said his father. "Have you?"

"Oh yes," replied the small boy, brightly. "It isn't bad really. You ought to try it."

A reader's letter to the Dalesman from June 1940:

"I am very glad you have been able to carry on. In peacetime the Dalesman was a treasure. In wartime it has been a blessing as well, and it is fast becoming, to me at any rate, almost a necessity."

IT WAS April 1941, and a schoolteacher was taking a class in literature. He quoted the lines

> *Oh, to be in England*
> *now that April's there*

and then asked "Who said that?"

The small boy who was questioned thought it over carefully for a moment and then replied:

"Hitler, sir."

"ALL THOSE who care for our rural life will welcome the marked revival this year [1945] of the agricultural shows throughout the Yorkshire countryside. From each of the three Ridings there has been news of successful revivals, and attendances have been surprisingly good.

"After all, not many months have elapsed since VE Day and a vast amount of organisation has had to be put in by officers and others. The excellent support they had from exhibitors speaks well for the future of our agricultural industry. We hope that next year will see a revival of the Great Yorkshire Show as well as bigger and better local shows in every dale.

"I only regret that the continuing limitation of our space have prevented us from giving a fuller picture of this notable revival of the Dales shows. By next year I sincerely hope that our paper ration will be more equal to our wishes."

Harry J Scott, editor

A 'townie' passing comment on Swaledale during a visit there said:

"There's an awful lot of countryside about."

A DALESMAN was always bothered about his health.

"I's goin' to try that acupuncture," he decided. "I've just sin an hedgehog and it seems to have worked alreet for it."

"SORRY TO hear you've lost your wife, Fred"

"Aye — she were a good 'un."

"What did she dee of?"

"I don't reetly knaa. It were one o' them queer complaints that tha doesn't know tha's got till tha's gone."

DURING THE Second World War a dalesman in the forces received letters from his sister complaining of the flightiness of his wife during his absence. Furthermore on his arrival home on leave his sisters greeted him with the obvious intention of fanning the flame which they had ignited. He forestalled them with:

"Nay, let's get one war ower, afore tha begins another."

He was left in peace.

A FARMER was asked his opinion of scarecrows.

"No good at all," he growled. "Leastways they don't work on t' crows round 'ere. Last year I put up a grand 'un — it were a man pointin' a gun."

"Well what happened?" he was asked.

"All t' crows in t' world came to feed in that field. One crow perched on t' gun and worked t' trigger, and another crow fell dahn and pretended to be shot."

A ROTHERHAM woman had never used teabags, so her friend decided to give her a box of them to make less work.

After a few weeks she called on the old woman and, in the course of conversation, asked her how she was doing with the teabags.

"Oh," replied the old lady, "The tea's varra good but I do find it a nuisance having to clip them li'le bags to get t' tea out."

"Have I passed?"

14

A CALDERDALE man's wife died. As her memorial be erected a large stone at the head of the grave. Across the stone were the words:

"The light of my life has gone out."

Very soon the village was surprised when he suddenly announced his engagement to another woman. A wag added a few words to the stone which read:

"But he struck another match."

Battery hens are OK, but the long-life ones are much better.

A HUSBAND and wife are on a walking and camping trip in the Dales. After a long day's hiking in beautiful sunshine, the couple pitch their tent in a stunning part of Wensleydale and, utterly exhausted, they soon fall sound asleep.

In the middle of the night, awoken by the screech of a passing owl, the woman shakes her husband's shoulder to wake him also.

"John, look up," she says. "What do you see?"

"Well, I see thousands of stars," he says, sleepily. "What a beautiful sky."

"And what does that mean to you?" his wife asks.

"Well, I suppose it means we are in for another nice day tomorrow. What does it mean to you?"

"Well John," she replies. "To me, it means someone's stolen our tent."

Old Yorkshire inns

Their quaint signs have swung through the ages
Well battered by wind and by rains,
You'll find them in quiet old hamlets,
You'll find them in old Yorkshire lanes —
The King's Head, the George and the Dragon,
The Mermaid, the Dun Cow, the Bell;
They all hide great history behind them,
They all have rare stories to tell;
There pilgrims and kings have found shelter,
And rough peasantry quaffed their beer,
With beggars, quacks and tipsy cheapjacks
And sociable folk of good cheer;
Yet still their signs swing through the ages —
The Black Bull, Red Lion, the Star —
A welcome sight on a storm-tossed night
To the ones who have travelled far.

Dorothy Morton

RACE MEETINGS are often noisy but colourful affairs. The Kiplingcotes Derby, England's oldest endowed race, is neither. The winning post bears the date of 1519, the year when traditionally the first race was run, but the first authentic record of a race meeting at Kiplington — or Kibling Coates as it was then called — seems to be in 1555 when it is mentioned in some court evidence in the diocesan archives at York.

Nowadays (1974) there is only one race, the Kiplingcotes Derby, and the conditions are the same as those imposed by the founders:

"A horse race is to be observed and ridd yearly on the third Thursday of March; open to horses of all ages, 10 stones exclusive of saddle, to enter at ye post, before eleven o'clock on the morning of ye race. The race to be run before two."

This race is unique but fascinating. It is run over a four-mile course without enclosures, paddock or tote, and there are no bookies to call the odds.

Nowadays the course is run along the old Roman road which connected with Brough and Malton and finishes across the A163, a little west of Middleton-on-the-Wold. A policeman holds up traffic on the Queen's Highway. The course is a muddy rubble track and a stiff test for any horse.

The race does show more than a touch of Tyke humour. The prize money is to say the least modest, and the horse which comes second receives more money than the winner

"Of course it's expensive — giant bonsai trees are very rare."

TWO MEN in a Settle pub were discussing weather conditions in the Three Peaks.

Said one: "There's allus thick mist on Whernside, except when it's a fine sunny day."

"Aye," said the other. "And on Ingleborough the mists are so thick, you can drive a nail into them and hang your 'at and coit on it."

YOUNG DAVID had been on a school trip to London to view the 'sights'. He was explaining to his father that they had visited the Law Courts:

"You know, dad, the place where they dispense with justice."

The *Dalesman* editor writes:

"THE SECOND World War has not changed our Dales. The high hills still take on their hues of purple and brown. The limestone still glistens in the spring sunshine and the white walls still spangle the brilliantly green pastures like a giant net thrown casually over the landscape. Spring still brings its old loveliness. But this loveliness has a new audience.

"In place of the walkers and cyclists and motorists has come a new company of visitors. Eighteen months ago we welcomed the first batch of a strange and wondrous army bearing the then name of 'evacuees'. Slowly that army drifted back to its native towns, a little puzzled by this country and saddened by its absence of 'entertainment'. That was before the word 'blitz' came into our speech.

"Now has come a new company of evacuees from Poland who for the most part have borne the strain and suffering of war at first hand, whose daily life has been lived to an accompaniment of raids and alarms, and to whom death and destruction have been a normal peril.

"To this company Dales folk have offered a real Yorkshire welcome, practical in its application and deep and genuine in its sincerity."

A TEACHER in a Dewsbury school had asked her class:

"Where does one find elephants?"

She did not expect the answer from one bright young lass:

"The elephant is such a girt big animal it nivver gits lost and it doesn't need findin'."

Dreams of yesterday

Down our little country lane, the 'great' steamroller came
And the smell of 'boiling tar', it filled the air,
But, it heralded 'bad news', as it stuck fast to our shoes,
And our poor hardworking mums, they all went 'spare'.

A white-coated gentleman used to drive the co-op van,
He was the only shop for 'miles' around,
A silver sixpence bought you sweets, toffee sticks and rosebud treats,
You could get a lot of groceries for a pound.

In the fields we used to play, whilst the sun shone all the day,
We'd pick mushrooms, blackberries, and bitter sloe.
Then inside the hessian sacks, we 'bagged' the crusty old cow pats,
And it didn't half make our roses grow.

We cycled miles on our bikes as the traffic then was light,
To the river, for a picnic and a swim.
Wild garlic, sweet primrose and scented violets lined the road,
Then we'd 'wend' our way back home as light got dim.

Now there's hardly any 'green', just houses where it's been,
And the traffic queues get 'bigger' down our way.
We've computers, mobile phones, all 'mod cons' in our homes,
But inside, I'll keep my 'dreams of yesterday'.

Heather Overfield

"I know she's a good milker — it's getting her into the stall that's the trouble."

A DEVOUT Methodist in the Skipton district was presented at intervals with five sons. The minister christened them Mark, Matthew, Luke and John. The Methodist then went to the minister to select the name for number five.

"What about the Five Apostles?" he asked.

Many brides go to the altar and most alter afterwards.

A DALES farmer was having trouble starting his car when a local lady wearing a big hat and who was a notorious scandalmonger came up to him and, smiling, said:

"I see you're having trouble with your new car."

"Aye," the farmer replied. "I nivver trusts anything under a bonnet."

Memories of a doctor in the Dales during wartime

"I AM doing temporary duty at the emergency hospital attached to this sanatorium. It consists of ten wards, several of which are not completely finished, wooden erections at present occupied by some 200 old people evacuated from London hospitals, institutions and homes in bombed areas.

"On Saturday morning we got orders to prepare for over 300 schoolchildren and teachers to arrive on Monday evening and depart to billets in homes in the Dales the following morning. The wards had to be made ready, beds and bedding to be procured, food to be got. The regular staff was supplemented by VAD nursing auxiliaries and St John Ambulance personnel.

"I went round the place before the children came. It looked really beautiful and attractive. A thirty-five-bed ward was made to hold sixty beds. The children began to arrive at 8pm after over 12 hours on the railway journey, all tired and hungry. By 10.30pm everyone had been washed, fed and bedded. At 2pm Tuesday, they went off to their various destinations in charas. There was not a single hitch and some said they wished they could 'stay here for keeps'.

"We hear so much quibbling and grousing about official red tape, I think it would be a pity not to let this little incident be known. It might at least help to cheer the parents whose children have to be evacuated."

AUNT POLLY, a spinster of the parish now in her late seventies, felt that she had reached the time of life when thoughts must turn to the inevitable. So she decided that she should make arrangements for her funeral, telling her friends and family that she had been beholden to no one all her life and was not planning to change now.

She went off to see the village undertaker to make the arrangements, and all went well until the time came to select the lining material for the coffin.

"Well," the undertaker explained, "we normally bury the married ladies with a lovely deep purple lining, but unwed ladies like thissen usually prefer to have a nice bit of white taffeta."

Aunt Polly pondered on this and then replied:

"Ah'll tell thee what. Tha can use the white taffeta — but tha can pipe the edges wi' purple, just ter let 'em know as Ah've 'ad mi moments."

A New Year's Resolution is one that goes in one year and out the other.

A LITTLE evacuee from London was brought from Keighley to a beautiful park at Oakworth. All at once she said to her hostess:

"This isn't England is it?"

"Yes it is — why?" was the reply.

"Because there is a war on in England and there isn't a war on here."

"Oh, that? That's for ringing for the butler."

AN AGED farmer near Halifax was wobbling home as usual after a 'neet at t' pub', and when he got home his wife was still working on the spring cleaning. He did not even see her as he staggered up to bed. His wife shouted:

"Thee mind that tha don't run into yon chest of drawers I's shifted on to t' landing."

The farmer grunted a drunken reply:

"It's nut goin' to run anyweer."

A TIGHT-FISTED farmer put half a crown on a collection plate at church by mistake. The following Sunday when the collection was being taken, he glared at the sidesman and said:

"It's reet — I'se gitten a season ticket."

A letter to a wartime friend:
"YOU MAY not know that Yorla Tank Corps is stationed at Ellerton. These days there is not a lane around where it is safe to lead a young 'oss. Tanks coom rattlin' along, bustin' through fields across intake making a fiersome din and cuttin' up roads summat cruel.

"They goes uphill and downdale same as if they were so many Jack Hares. How somiver on top of this hill aboot here is an ack-ack station and when guns start boomin — they don't half shek my cottage I can tell you.

Last week they had a party of ENSAs from London to give them a show in their girt hut. There was a funny man, with a serious face, and a tap dancer with nobbut little feet. She wore white clogs, then there were a lass with fluffed-oot red hair what played the pianner and sang soprano with a high voice.

"The all come in a van like a horse box, the tap dancer and the soprano sat inside with the pianner, and the funny man sat alongside another girl wot drove. She looked as if a puff of wind would blow her away, but she managed that 'oss box with the best of them. The pianner got a bad fall as two soldiers were lifting it oot o' t' 'oss box, which didn't do it no good."

J B Priestley's memories of a Yorkshire Christmas in the days before the First World War:

"CHRISTMAS IN those days was far less of a commercial rocket to boost the winter trade, but more a hearty and widespread enjoyment of the season itself. Brass bands played and carols were sung in the streets. You visited dozens of houses where rich cakes and mince pies were washed down with beer, port, whisky and rum the air was fragrant and thick with cigar smoke, whole warehouses of presents were exchanged, and shops overflowed with turkeys, geese, hams, puddings, candied fruit, figs, dates, chocolate, holly and coloured and gilded paper hats. There has been nothing like it since and probably will not be again. We Yorkshire people celebrated Christmas in a huge, rich, leisurely way."

"Don't bother telling Father Christmas about me wanting a bike," a young lad told his mum.

"Why not?" he was asked.

"Cos I've just found one in t' wardrobe."

A LEYBURN man bought a new piano and two days later he was seen wheeling it around in a handcart.

"What's up wi yon pianner?" he was asked.

"Nowt," was the reply "Ahm just off for a lesson."

TIMMY FEATHER, the last of the handloom weavers, was at his cottage door feeding hens and after a brief chat he said:

"Cum in an' I'll wayve ye a pick or two."

We went upstairs, where I found his bed covered with what appeared to be old sacking, and the handloom taking up most of the remaining space. He slid on the bench, seized the cross beam — the slay bar I think he called it — and presently the loom sprang into action.

But Timmy could talk as well as weave, and presently, he was in a flood of reminiscences, the tales he told being rich in the dialect.

He recalled the time when a new-fangled thing called a railway had been opened up in the valley below. Being men of spirit they decided to try the new thing. So in due course, with their woven pieces over their backs, instead of taking the usual route to their market in Halifax they strode off to Hebden Bridge. They then boarded the train, which were then little less than open trucks.

And at this point in the narrative the clacking ceased and Timmy slewed on his seat to give emphasis to his words, reliving those adventurous moments.

"Shoo bumped and shoo banged and shoo rattled," he said, "an' there wer smoke and steam ivverwheer".

A tunnel frightened the travellers, and at Sowerby Bridge they promptly dismounted and tramped it to Halifax, glad to be still alive and on their feet, which was the form of transport which they trusted most.

Yule logs

Beechwood fires are bright and clear,
If the logs are kept a year;
Chestnut only good we say,
If for long it's laid away;

Make a fire of elder tree —
Death within your house shall be;
But ash new, or ash old
Is fit for queen with crown of gold.

Birch and fir logs burn too fast,
Blaze up bright but do not last;
It is by the Irish said,
Hawthorn bakes the sweetest bread.

Elmwood burns like churchyard mould —
E'en the very flames are cold;
But ash green or ash brown
Is fit for queen with golden crown.

Poplar gives a bitter smoke,
Fills your eyes and makes you choke;
Applewood will scent your room
With an incense-like perfume.

Oaken logs if dry and old,
Keep away the winter's cold;
But ash wet or ash dry,
A king shall warm his slippers by.

THE INFANTS class had been learning all about sums and the different words for them.

"What is the total?" the teacher asked.

"The total," replied one little boy, "is what you get when you add up all the numbers."

"And what is the remainder?" the teacher then asked.

"The remainder, miss, is the animal wot pulls Santa's sleigh."

TWO OLD ladies were at prayers in a Bingley church. One whispered to the other:

"Ee, Ellen, I passed thy cottage and you'd left t' key in t' front door."

"That's reet," was Ellen's reply, "but there's nowt to worry about — Ah locked it."

"AT THE other end of our row of houses was Alfred Smith's bakery, which was also the post office and general stores, run by a family called Baldwin who had a small field close by and kept a few hens and ducks, two big fat turkeys and two geese.

"As Christmas 1934 came, I think they decided to do us a good turn because, by some strange quirk of fate, one of the geese got its head caught in the drinking-trough and strangled itself, so they asked my dad if we would mind having it for Christmas dinner. They already had a turkey and, anyway, the goose was rather a pet so they couldn't bring themselves to eat it. I don't know whether dad believed their sad story but it was a nice big goose and a good Christmas dinner for us. What a silly old goose!

"Now on Christmas Eve 1934, John and I heard our parents go next door to the Holroyds for a drink, so we nipped down to see our presents on the table. A blow football game wasn't wrapped so we had a game or two — until we heard everyone shouting 'Merry Christmas', then we bundled it back into its box and shot off back to bed. It would have been a disaster if they'd found the jumbled-up mess and the now-wet tubes; they'd have known we didn't believe in Santa Claus.

"I believed in Santa for another three or four years because I also knew you got less for Christmas when you no longer believed in the Magic of Christmas… Sneaky!"

Ernest Astley

A PUB quiz in a Dales hostelry has reached a tie-break, with nothing to separate two of the regulars. The duo are told that the winner will be the first to name three fish beginning with the letter K. After a moment's hesitation, one of the men replies:

"Killer shark, kippered herring and Kettlewell."

"What do you mean? Kettlewell isn't a fish," the landlord exclaims.

"Aye 'tis," the man retorts, "it's a place".

"THOO SHOULD see my tonnips," declared the boastful farmer. "There some so big I can't lift 'em mysel. We managed to git some on 'em to t' sheep i' bad weather. Then one day we'd a sheep missing. But when we cut up t' tonnips, theer in t' middle o' one on 'em was t' yow that were missing."

"That lass o' John's is a bonny girl, but Ah reckon when she made her face up she thinks she's dressed."

A LAD was starting work on a farm on the North York Moors which kept turkeys.

"How can you tell the age of a turkey?" he was asked.

The reply came quickly. "By the teeth."

"But birds don't have teeth" said the farmer.

"I knows, but I have," replied the lad.

WE WILL refrain from mentioning the Yorkshire football ground on which this happened, but the home team was playing very badly during an evening kick-off, and there were caustic comments from the suppporters:

"They're playing like a load o' kids."

"This lot couldn't laik dominoes."

"Get 'em a nursemaid."

were just some of the comments. Then a lone voice rang out:

"Get some new players."

"Aye, but they can't find 'em," replied a disconsolate spectator. "What do you think floodlights is on for but to look for 'em?"

On her way home on the school bus, a young lass was singing to herself. The conductor, who was not familiar with the words, asked her what she was singing. The little lass replied:

"Them words is my own composure."

A FAMILY with a teenage son were camping in the Yorkshire Wolds. The father had agreed to give his son a driving lesson on the quiet lanes near the campsite. They had not gone far when the mother, who was watching from nearby, signalled violently for them to stop.

"Don't take everything with you," she yelled.

Father and son looked behind them. There, attached to the car by the washing line that had been tied to the rear bumper, were the tent, several buckets and the week's washing.

THE TEACHER had taken the infants class on a school trip to the Brontë Parsonage, and was delighted to note how the youngsters absorbed all the details. When the group stopped in the sitting room for a moment, the teacher said in an awed voice:

"Isn't it wonderful to think that Charlotte, Emily and Ann Brontë sat in that chair."

One little lad reached out and put his hand on the chair, and declared in a loud whisper:

"They must have just left — it's still warm."

We just had *to get back to the simple life."*

AT THE bar of a Wakefield pub, two friends were discussing the new girlfriend of a mutual acquaintance:

"She's alreet till she oppens 'er mouth, but she's got a reyt queer twang."

WHEN TOLD by his vicar that the meek would inherit the earth, an old Nidderdale man replied with a grunt:

"When time comes for t' meek to inherit the Earth, the taxes will be so great that they waint want it."

AN OLD dalesman was asked if he wanted electricity installing in his farmhouse. Cables were being laid close to his premises and the Electricity Board called to see if he wanted his house to be linked to the National Grid. He agreed, but only up to a point, as he explained:

"I'll have a light on t' landing; it'll shine into all t' bedrooms so there's neea need for lights in ivvery room. Put a switch on t' landing light, so as when we switch off at night, we can use oor candles to light oor way ti bed."

HULL CITY were playing at home and not doing very well. One of the forwards was injured and his retirement to the dressing room seemed inevitable. A substitute was ready and, wearing a tracksuit, was sprinting up and down the touchline as a warm-up prior to being ordered onto the pitch. This went on for some time, until there was a shout from one anxious supporter:

"Tha'd better git thisel onto t' pitch, owd lad, or thee'll tire theesel out afowre that gits a kick o' t' ball."

A Reeth child was asked at Christmas where Jesus was born. With a gleam in his eye the lad replied:
"Under an 'olly bush."

"LIKE ALL children we looked forward to Christmas. We didn't get much in the way of toys but we hung our socks in hope.

I got a celluloid doll, very popular in the 1930s but flammable if too near the fire. Mine was rescued from the hearth just in time, but not before it had partially melted. It was a very authentic-looking hospital case when we played nurses.

"As the older end of the family got jobs, things eased financially for my mother. We had a goose on Christmas Day and its grease was put to a surprising number of uses — on shoes to keep them waterproof, on chapped hands and knees, on creaking doors, wheezy chests and for cooking. Ugh!

"We pooled our pennies from carol singing to get something for mam and dad. Mam liked dark chocolate and dad usually got hankies with his initials on.

"Sitting in the firelight listening to our parents reminiscing on Christmases past was a time to be savoured. We never wanted Dad's stories to end. We'd say 'Then what happened?' just to keep him going."

Mary Pickard

THE REV Tiverton Preedy was a man of all the talents. Obviously he was deeply religious, but also an accomplished pianist, a talented footballer and a boxer with a good punch. This fighting man of cloth became vicar of St. Peter's Church in Barnsley but he was ambitious for the football club. As usual this man of energy was the driving force and the Oakwell pitch became the home of Barnsley FC. This cost money and so the 'boxing priest' solved the problem after formation on 6th September 1887 by charging an admission fee of three old pence. In 1897 there was a debate which resulted in the church reference being dropped and it has been Barnsley FC ever since.

The club played in the FA Cup Finals of 1910 and 1912. When northerners were 'up fer t' Cup' the southern people did not take kindly to their rough speech and strange sense of humour. Apart from rattles, scarves, hats the club had a mascot: the famous Amos the Donkey.

On going smokeless

My atlas has a weather map
  That portions out the Sun;
Red for the counties where it shines
  And white for those with none.

For sixteen hundred hours a year
  It beats on Beachy Head,
But Bradford and the Aire must do
  With barely twelve instead.

Dorset and Kent look nicely baked
  And Exmoor and the Weald,
But the shading turns a paler hue
  From York to Huddersfield.

Well, never mind; the map may soon
  Give us a redder tone
When Keighley down to Doncaster
  Is one big smokeless zone.

We've done our bit; it's coke from now
  Or pure electric heat;
We'll have the laugh when it's non-stop Sun
  From Leeds to Simons Seat.

Brass without muck and sunlit moors,
  Blue skies the whole year through;
We'll show them yet in Somerset
  What Yorkshire suns can do.

R S Smith

A MINISTER was giving a sermon in a Dales village when he said:

"Man doth not live by bread alone."

A woman stood up and marched out."

"Wot's up wi thee?" the minister shouted.

"Its all reet, tha's just reminded me I've left two tattie pies in t' oven."

A YOUNG farmer was coming home from market with a young pig under each arm. He was about to pass a young woman who speeded up.

"What's thi hurry?" he asked.

"Ah thowt thi were going to kiss me."

"How can I do that when I'm carrying two pigs?"

"Ah thowt tha might ask me to hold thy pigs," said the ever-hopeful lass.

An apology from the editor of Dalesman, *July 1944:*
"I MUST apologise for the very unfortunate delay in publication which meant the late arrival of the magazine last month. Our printers explain that their paper suppliers had their stocks requisitioned and for nearly a fortnight they were awaiting new supplies. Meanwhile we could do nothing but gaze at the proofs of the delayed issue and listen to the thump of angry letters through the letterbox from justifiably indignant readers. I hope the time is not far off when we shall be free from the 'alarums and excursions' of this sort and we will be able to ensure the smooth running of this little magazine in a way that has been impossible during the last five years."

The call of the Dales

by Lieut E P Mallinson, HMS Hermione
(written in 1942)

O 'twill be good to be striding the Dales again
When peace is finally won:
Knowing our efforts have not been in vain
And the reign of goodwill has begun.

To step into the wind and the sun and the sky
With a song of lonely places;
With a faith so rich and a courage so high
That the spirit the flesh outpaces

To hear curlew and redshank and wild mallard duck
Screaming shouts of derisive defiance
As you traverse their wild, waste lands and look
To vast void for the lark's cadence.

To drop down from the hills as the murk of dusk
Steals silently over the uplands,
To the little villages, cradled and hushed
In the quiet of the dalelands.

Yes it will be good to have tramped the dales again
From sunrise, thro' sunshine to starlight;
To return once again to the haunts of men,
In a world at peace and enlightened.

The five seasons of the Dales in 1944

DALESFOLK REMEMBER the joys of seeing, hearing, smelling, tasting and feeding. Many of these sensations have been long forgotten or we are too busy to notice.

Seeing:
Cloud shadows chasing upon open hill country.
The blue shadows of sunlit snow.
A full moon bathing the roofs of a sleeping village.

Hearing:
The running waters on rocky streams.
The distant noise of railway trains, now puffing and clanking up, now rattling down, a long incline.
The piping and crying of curlews.

Smelling:
Heather in full bloom on a dry, warm day.
In the fields: broad beans in flower; new-mown hay.

Tasting:
A farmhouse tea of home-cured ham and eggs.
Well-matured Yorkshire parkin.

Feeling:
A wet west wind when walking on the high hills.
The glow of the face, neck and hands after a long day out in the sun and the wind.

Most of this costs little or nowt, and so does exploring Nature.

"Have you found any needles yet?"

AT HARLOW Carr Gardens, a man came into the shop for some potted geraniums.

"Sorry, we have run out of geraniums," the shop assistant told him. "But won't these fine chrysanthemums do instead?"

"No good," the man replied. "They must be geraniums. They are to replace some I promised to look after while the wife was away."

OLD NELLIE, very deaf and weak of sight, wanted a TV set. When it was pointed out to her that, as there was no electricity supply to her remote cottage, it would be useless, the stubborn old lady brusquely retorted:

"Then git me yan that'll work by gas."

A FARMER on a wet and windy night saw a light moving across his farmyard. Thinking it might be a poacher, he investigated and instead found his hired hand.

"We-er ist thou goin' wi' a lantern?" he asked.

"I's off courtin".

"When I were thy age I didn't use a lantern."

"I kna," replied the lad "I realised that when I saw thy missus."

A lady living near Doncaster was talking about railway accidents. Her husband commented:

"The most dangerous place is in the last carriage."

"Reet, then — why don't they leave the last one off?"

SOME OF the funniest tales have arisen through the dalesman's attempts to cope with modern technology, or what they term 'new-fangled contraptions'. It is not that many years ago that the telephone was in that category. Back in those days, a Dales farmer had to ring the vet as one of his pigs was ill, so he went to the telephone box in the village. A notice in the kiosk read '1d, 6d, 3s'; the farmer thought it was a list of charges and so he decided to have the cheapest on offer.

When the operator asked him what number he

required, he said it wasn't a number he was wanting, "It's yon vet. Tell 'im that oor pig's ailing and 'e 'as ti git there quick."

The operator then tried to explain that she had no idea which vet he was trying to contact, whereupon the farmer exclaimed:

"That un that cums tiv oor farm ivvery Tuesday."

In an attempt to establish some kind of contact with the caller, the operator asked him for his name and where he lived.

"Yon vet knows where Ah live," he replied tersely. "Just tell 'im ti git 'imself 'ere quick afore that pig o' mine pegs oot."

HORSE RACING was always a place to find a generous slice of Yorkshire humour. After failing to find a winner, a disgruntled punter was drowning his sorrows in a Wetherby pub.

"So you picked a slow un, did yer?" asked the landlord.

"Aye — one that were so slow that t' jockey took a packed lunch."

A MOTORIST was driving across the Wolds. He was behind a tractor at the time. Suddenly, without warning or a signal of any kind, the tractor driver turned into a field. The motorist had to drive into a ditch to avoid a collision, and he promptly remonstrated with the tractor driver, whose reply was:

"It's my farm so it's my field, and I allus turn in here."

"Ah allus keeps a couple o' goats to 'elp clear up t' picnic litter."

AN INQUISITIVE American visitor to Grassington came up to a farmer and pointed to his shiny new car.

"What is this?" he asked.

"It's a car," replied his astonished listener.

"We call it an automobile," smiled the American.

The farmer pointed to his scythe standing up against a wall.

"What does tha call that?" he asked.

"We call it a scythe," replied the American.

"Dust tha?" said the farmer. "Round 'ere we calls it an automograss, but it doesn't. It's a bit like thee — not quite sharp enough."

EIGHT-YEAR-old Lucy had been asked by her teacher to write down what was so good about grandmothers:

"A grannie is a lady who has no children of her own and so loves the boys and girls of other people.

"Grannies have nothing to do. They only have to be there. If they take you for a walk they go slowly and past lovely leaves and caterpillars. They never say 'Come along quickly' or 'Hurry up for goodness sake'.

"They are usually fat, but not too fat to tie up your shoelaces. They wear glasses, and sometimes take their teeth out. They answer questions like 'Why do dogs hate cats?' and 'Why isn't God married?'. They never mind reading the same story over and over again.

"Everyone should have a grannie and especially those who have no internet. Grannies are the only grown-ups who always have time."

Seen written in the grime on the back of a particularly dirty Land Rover at Skipton auction mart:

"Don't wash me: plant summat."

OLD TOM had driven a bus around the Whitby district for years, and was notorious for giving his passengers a bumpy ride. On one occasion the bumps were worse than usual and the passengers shouted complaints. One old lady shouted back:

"Thee leave him be. He's just cured mi lumbago."

AT A meeting of Yorkshiremen in London some years ago, one man remarked how well he knew the County of Broad Acres and especially Ilkley. A hitherto unobserved man in a corner piped up:

"Tha'll knaw Ben Rhyddin' then?"

Flummoxed, he replied:

"Well, er, yer see, Ah didn't kna Ben so weel as 'is other brothers."

The theories of modern science, as expounded by a Bridlington schoolboy:

"Electricity and lightning are the same thing, except that lightning is several miles long while electricity is only a few inches."

A YORKSHIRE horse deal was never a very speedy operation, and often several hours elapsed before the money and the horse changed hands. One man sold a horse with the comment:

"I'm afraid it doesn't look so good."

"Looks all reight to me," said the buyer.

But the buyer was back a few hours later.

"That hoss you selled me's blind i' one eye," he declared.

"Aye," said the dealer, "I told thee it didn't look soa good."

ON A bitterly cold morning, a man is fishing at a partly frozen beck in upper Wharfedale, with little success. After a while, a boy arrives and starts fishing himself, a little further upstream. Within minutes he catches a huge brown trout. To the man's astonishment, just five minutes later, he lands another. This continues apace, with fish after fish being pulled from the stream and, after a while, the man can contain his curiosity no longer. He walks up the beck and asks the boy what his secret is.

"Yu hf tu kp yr wms wm," the youngster replies.

"Sorry? I didn't catch that," says the man, at which point the boy turns and spits something into a bucket.

"I said, 'yer have t' keep yer worms warm'."

THE SPORT of quoits is still played in a few places in the North of England. The game is played on a pitch, eleven yards from hob to hob. The hob, or pin, is a short metal rod, four or five inches high, set in the centre of a square yard of clay, the rest of the pitch being concrete or just grass.

The quoit weighs five pounds and is made of steel. It is specially constructed, being thin at the outer edge and thicker at the inner edge. One surface is rounded and the other flat — they are called 'hill' and 'hole'.

A team consists of nine men; it used to be eleven and still is in a few districts. The two teams meet on the quoits pitch and the opposing pairs are decided by drawing their names out of a hat. The first pair commence, after tossing up to decide who throws first. They do not toss a coin, but a quoit and the cry is 'hill or hole'. Each man has two quoits and they throw alternately, staring at one hob, running two paces, then aiming at the other hob.

A quoit that encircles the hob is a 'ringer' and counts two points unless it is 'topped', that is, covered by the opponent's quoit. If the four quoits score no 'ringers' the nearest quoit counts one point. Often a pair of callipers will be produced to ensure the accuracy of measurement.

The sound of quoits ringing is still one of the pleasantest sounds in a village on a summer's evening. These old innkeepers knew a thing or two about salesmanship; they only had to provide a quoits pitch and the game would ensure plenty of thirsty customers.

IN THE game of 'oily marbles' the focal point for the marbles was a hole in the ground about the size of a tennis ball.

To open the game, each player in turn tossed an equal number of marbles towards the hole. Then the owner of the marble judged to be nearest to the hole took first turn at trying to steer the marble into the hole, using a forward nudging movement with the side of his crooked forefinger. One marble, one nudge. If successful with the first marble, he continued by trying the next marble, and so on until he failed to nudge one into the hole; at which point he claimed all the marbles in the hole. The next player, judged by the nearness of his 'tans' to the hole, then followed in like manner until the pitch was cleared.

'Ringy Marbles' is the Harrogate version of 'oily'. It called for each player to place an agreed number of marbles inside a ring chalked on the ground. The players then tossed a large marble (usually called a 'glass ally') towards the ring. The player with his ally at rest nearest to the ring took first turn at trying to knock marbles out of the ring, aiming from the point at which his ally stood.

With practice, a trigger-like action of the thumb against the forefinger (in the crook of which the ally was placed) produced quite an effective shot.

Any marbles knocked out were 'won', but after an ineffective shot the ally had to remain on the 'pitch', this becoming a potential target for his mates who, by hitting it, could knock the ally owner out of the game.

A THIXENDALE farmer, asked by a visitor if he owned a horse, replied "We hev' hoaf o' yan", meaning that he share a horse with a neighbouring farmer.

The visitor, a 'townie', thinking he would make the local sound foolish, asked:

"And which half do you own?"

Realising that he was being taken for a ride, the farmer replied:

"Oh, we hev t' back hoaf — it gives t' muck and dun't want feedin'."

"My advice is keep off foie gras, caviar and champagne."

A YOUNG man from the city thought he would like a country job for a change and went to call on a farmer.

"Well," said the farmer, "I don't know what a city man could do here. What were you?"

"I was a fitter-mechanic."

"Do you think you could shoe a horse?"

"Well," said the mechanic, "I'm willing to try."

"All right, I've got to go into the village for an hour or so. See what you can make of the job."

When the farmer returned he found the horse lying on its back, with all four feet stuck in the air. It had been shod, though, and the job had been well done.

"You've made a good fist of that," he complimented, "but what's matter with the horse? He looks a bit odd."

"I've been worrying about that," replied the mechanic. "He's been like that ever since I took him out of the vice."

Overheard at a bus stop in Wakefield:

"I knew Job had his trials, but he never had to make seven more payments on a car that lost an argument with a lorry."

A WENSLEYDALE farmer was complaining to a neighbour about the poor quality of modern-day clothing, illustrating his point by saying:

"Ah nobbut had these trousers ten year an' t' buttons are comin' off."

A Dalesman poacher

Ah used ter tak me rod an' net
When t' river ran just reight
Ah knew a spot where monny a trout
Put up a bonny feight.

Ah'd so am' stare at t' watter theer
An' see a gurt 'un jump;
A silver flash — a plop — an' rings
Me hear fair used ter thump!

An' nah Ah've found another place
Wi' ivv'rything yer'd wish.
A level bank, a handy bush,
An' watter full o' fish.

Ah tak' me line an' bait, an' hooks,
But not me rod — no fear.
It wi'n't goa in me pocket, see …
Its 'Private Fishing' theer.

Will Clemence

A FARM labourer was leading a horse down a road where two ladies in their car left him insufficient room to pass. He told them so — bluntly.

After a complaint his farmer employer told him to apologise. So in the evening he called upon the ladies. Standing before them, cap in hand, he asked them if they were the two ladies he had told to go to hell when he passed them in the morning.

"Yes, we are," they said.

"Well, I've come to tell yer, yer needn't go."

KEITH WAS applying for a position with an industrial concern near Castleford. A bright young man presented him with an application form to fill in. When it came to the blank space for the age, Keith hesitated for a moment, so the young man remarked:

"Now hurry up — every minute makes it worse."

IN A South Yorkshire pub the topic of discussion was the European Union. One man summed it up:

"Ah reckon it's like this: we send 'em our products and in return they take our money."

AT A time when Keighley was producing some of the finest textile machinery in the world, one factory owner was interviewing a young man for an apprenticeship. The lad was asked if he could work with a 'mike' (micrometer) and a vernier (a kind of scale).

"Aye," said the lad, "I can work wi' any lad providing he is sociable."

ONE SHROVE Tuesday a mother was preparing pancakes for her sons, Kevin, five, and Sam, four. The siblings began to argue over who would get the first. Spotting an opportunity for a moral lesson, their mother told them:

"If Jesus were sitting here, he would say, 'Let my brother have the first pancake, I can wait'."

Quick as a flash, Kevin turned to his younger brother and said:

"Sam, you be Jesus."

After the brass band's big night out, one of the bandsmen was forced to place a small ad in the local paper:

"Has anyone seen our big drum? A reward will be given to the finder."

A FARMHAND named John was instructed by his employer to bury a sheep in the far field.

"You may as well clip her," said the farmer. "Take those shears and a sack with you."

John arrived back at the farm late for dinner. After a while the farmer asked:

"Did you manage all right, John?"

"Yes," said John.

"Then where is the wool?" asked the farmer.

"Oh," said John, "I put that in first."

THESE DAYS cars are produced by a very few number of companies but this was not always the case. Around 1900 there were many companies and some were hand-built in Yorkshire. Who has ever heard of the 4-cylinder 30-horsepower Hallamshire which was made in Sheffield? And what about the Critchley Motor Engineering Company built in Saltburn? Only two were built! This car may have been inspired by the 1908 motor speed trials which were held at Saltburn.

Writing in the 1960s, J H Baines remembered these times:

"I first drove a car in 1903 but the first I owned was a 1907 6-horsepower single-cylinder two-seater Gladiator car. Even in those days this had a detachable cylinder head and an automatic inlet valve. There were three speeds and a reverse, chain drive, water-cooled, water-pump friction driven off the flywheel. The radiator was fitted between the front wheels. The engine controls on this car, like most of this period, were hand levers for air, throttle and ignition.

"Further interesting features of the old cars were the external brakes on the rear wheels which became badly scored by the dirt and grit from the road. They had a foot brake and the brake shoes were on a drum at the back of the gearbox. The wooden wheels creaked badly in hot, dry weather and the cure was a liberal dose of water from the hosepipe which was fitted.

There was a road tax at this time; for vehicles up to 2 tons in weight it was £2 2s and for over 4 tons in weight this was doubled."

YOU DON'T realise how our meteorologists have played us false. They tell us that there are four, six or even eight types of wind. Don't believe it. There are many and some are maddening. There's the kneecap-knipper (a special affliction of women and schoolboys in short pants which almost justifies the wearing of slacks). Then there's the earlobe-lash, with a crack like a circus ringmaster's riding whip; the hamstring-howler; and the kidney-cringer, the one that remains in gleeful hiding until you try to light a pipe. Neither can you forget the lazy wind, that goes through you rather than round you.

Overheard in a Hull pub during a heated discussion on politics:
"Wot's a coil-ignition government?"

"WHILST STAYING in the Dales over Christmas in 1953 I was introduced to an unusual food called 'yoghourt'. It was made from soured milk and is, I understand, a valuable medicine much used by European peasants. I gather someone advertised it in your magazine a few years ago."
(The advertiser mentioned was Yalacta Ltd of Shipley)

OVERHEARD ON a Leeds bus:
"Wah washee wee woeshee wee her sen?"
This was not an advert for a Chinese restaurant. This was an old lady asking:
"Who was she with — was she by herself?"

"What shall I catch first, salmon or trout?"

THERE WAS a miner near Castleford who had a huge mouth. One of his mates said:

"If 'e'd any more gob, 'e'd 'ev no face to wesh."

A THRIFTY old daleswoman revisited Leyburn market to return a packet of soft toilet rolls. On demanding a refund the shopkeeper asked:

"Whats wrong with 'em?"

"Nowt" was the reply, "but the posh friends we was expecting nivver turned up. We can't afford stuff like that ourselves."

WHEN I was a lad at Ingleton forty years ago [wrote a dalesman in 1950] we used to receive visits from a vagabond who travelled under the name of 'Tin Whistle Bob'. He would assemble a crowd on the square and give a dramatic description of a railway locomotive driver's journey from Hellifield to Carlisle. There was much walking up and down, and the tin-whistle was much in evidence. After this the hat was passed round and the results produced a glorious drunk.

A DALESMAN commenting upon a strict teetotaller.
    "Ee's daft," he laughed. "I'm a carpenter and he dun't like me using a spirit level."

A Halifax man's opinion of a nosy lady:
    "I calls this woman Peninsular. A long neck sticking out to see."

A SWALEDALE farmer loved playing whist for high stakes. He had two city gentlemen staying at his farm. They played for £100 which would be paid if the farmer and his son won. If the visitors won they could take a sheep from his flock. The city men won and were told:
    "Tha can go out an' git thi own sheep in t' mornin'."
    The city men proved unable to catch the sheep and asked the farmer to help.
    "Nah" he replied "that weren't t' bargain. Thee go and get thi own and I'll charge thee board till tha gets it."
    The townies went home without the sheep.

RAISING A toast at a public meeting in Huddersfield, the host called out:

> *"All people that on earth do dwell*
> *Hold up thi hand and help thisell."*

IN THE 1930s a dalesman bought his first wireless set and told his grandma that he could get all the foreign stations. One night he was twiddling with the dials. Suddenly he felt a pain in his back and shouted to his grandma:

"I've gotten lumbago."

"Well it meks no odds," she replied. "Tha won't understand a word of it in a foreign twang."

Do lighthouse keepers enjoy a beacon sandwich?

A Bradford man visited Bolton Abbey ruins for the first time and exclaimed:

"Nay wunder t' munks won't live 'ere — jus' look at t' state they let t' place git into."

THE AIREDALE vicar's wife was calling on a small girl's mother.

"And how are you?" the vicar's wife enquired.

"Very well, thank you," replied the little girl.

"Now," said the visitor, "you should ask how I am."

Back came the reply:

"But I don't want to know."

'SANDSTONE JOHNNY' was one of Coverdale's humblest but most noted characters. He was so well known by his nickname that few dalesfolk could immediately recall his proper name of John Wilkinson.

His odd way of making a living was chiefly by the sale of scouring stones, which he collected near Rover Cragg, on Coverdale Moors, some 1,500 feet above sea-level.

He lived at West Scrafton and walked two miles up the moors, for the scouring sandstones, doing this journey regularly, filling his sack with as much as he could carry, probably about three stones in weight, then travelled not only Coverdale, but also a good deal of Wensleydale.

His usual price for a piece of scouring stone was a penny, small stones might be two or three for a penny, but he was never known to give any away and he would carry all the unsold stones back to his home.

He hated the motorcar and would walk into ditches to avoid one of "these new-fangled contraptions".

THERE WAS uproar in the kitchen of a Filey hotel. Voices were raised in fierce argument, and there was much thumping on the table. The hotelier hurried down to investigate and reached the kitchen just as the voices reached a deafening climax.

"What's all this shouting about?" he asked.

"If you please, sir," replied a red-faced scullery maid, "me an' t' cook's not speaking."

THE BESOM, the brush made of ling (heather stems) or birch twigs, is now only used in the farmyard, the cow-shed or the garden.

When all house floors were laid with stone flags and before carpets were anything but a luxury, the flags were kept clean by sprinkling them with sharp sand which, being ground underfoot, scoured the flags to a polish. The sand was made by 'braying' down the coarse sand-stone brought in from the moor and sold by the 'scouring stone men'. Every few days the old sand was swept out using a hard-wearing, old-fashioned besom.

At that time the demand for besoms meant that whole families could be employed. The skills needed to make a good besom was passed on from father to son, and three things are vital: there is ling or heather (*Calluna vulgaris*) for the head; ash for the binding; and hazel, ash, or other available timber for the handle.

In March the selected ling is either pulled or cut, the former being the more general practice. Selected 'ling bobs' are pulled up by the roots and the soil beaten off.

On the outskirts of the village of Wilsden and close to the moors is a pub called the Ling Bob which obviously takes us back to the time of the besom makers.

At that time whole families helped in the craft as this old rhyme indicates:

> *"Old Jamie's makkin besoms*
> *An' Jackie's rivin' spells;*
> *Dinah's fotchin' watter*
> *Fra t' owd spring wells."*

"I WAS born in Bradford in 1921 during the reign of George V and Queen Mary, when Lenin still ruled in Russia, but I was lucky to spend most of my young life in the countryside at Menston in Wharfedale.

"Milk than was delivered by horse and cart and ladled into a jug you left overnight on the doorstep, when all your groceries orders were delivered in a large cardboard box on a Friday evening. You had coal fires and paraffin heaters for warming the house. I remember at Menston we only had gas lighting for about a year, before electricity reached our grove. We had two deliveries of post daily and telephone boxes were plentiful with those Press buttons A and B.

"Christmas was quite different and perhaps in some way happier. Children didn't have the big expectations — or disappointments — and was less costly for parents. My first Christmas present was a two-foot long horse and cart and another time I got a metal car with headlights which lit up by a battery concealed underneath. The remaining presents were simple items — sweets, crayons, 'snap' cards, torches and books.

"Lighting on the Christmas tree was provided by coloured two-inch-long wax candles, which slotted into a small metal device and then clipped on to the tree's branches. No artificial trees or 'elf and safety' regulations then."

Mick Crossley

A WETHERBY man remembered the day when the 'thunder boxes' or outside toilets were replaced by flushing WCs at his school. Some years ago he worked as a plumber's merchant in the town.

"I must have sold thousands of WCs over the years and the different makes are a part of our social history. Who remembers Twyfords, Armitage Shanks, Howies, Southhooks, Howson, Royal Stevenson, Royal Venton and Ideal Standard Doulton?"

Overheard during a cold spell:
    "This is t' cowdest day we've had this year — and yesterday were even worse."

IT WAS one of the wettest years in the Broad Acres since records began. Arthur and Margaret were stoical about the dreary weather at first, but as the rains continued they became more and more fed up. When Cousin Bertha from Australia rang up, she was quite sympathetic about it all.

"All that rain," Bertha says. "Arthur must be taking it badly."

"Badly?" says Margaret. "Why I've never seen him so narked. He's takken it so bad, he says that if it rains any more, we might as well be living in Lancashire."

What did we go back to before the drawing board?

"Here we are ... Leeds Town Planning office — it's in Bradford."

A VICAR was on his bike on a snowy Thursday morning when he slipped and fell into a deep ditch. This was too steep to get out and he called two farmhands to help.

"Nay parson — tha can stay theer. Tha's no wanted till Sunday."

A YOUNG lad from Leeds went on a school trip to London. He was asked what he found out about the capital. He thought for a minute and said:

"Buckingham Palace needs a reet good wesh."

A CHILD from Bradford was asked by her teacher to explain the meaning of 'delta'.

"It's a river wi' its mouth full o' mud," was the reply.

A VICAR in Nidderdale paid his weekly visit to the church school for his usual question-and-answer session.

"What does God do?" he asked one little chap.

There was a pause before he replied.

"He saves our Gracious Queen."

IN THE old days in Yorkshire the most popular visitor was the rent collector. Most people said to him:

"We should be glad if you would call again later."

THESE DAYS local salmon is an expensive item on the menu, but in the Sedbergh area the fish was once so common that apprentices had a clause in their indentures that they would not have salmon for their dinner more than three days a week.

THE GENERATION gap — father to son:

"When I were your age I started work at five in the mornin' an thowt nowt of it."

"You were reet there, dad — I don't think much of it either."

A HECKMONDWIKE woman told a friend her husband had stopped smoking after forty years.

"Eeh, but it'd tak some will-power," said the friend.

"It did — and I've plenty of it."

"I told it to "eel"."

A BILSDALE farmer's wife had a low opinion of supermarket sausages.

"I allus meks me own," she commented.

"Do you put bread in them?" asked her friend.

"Nah, nobbut meat. Tha can allus put a slice o' bread wee 'um once they've bin cooked."

A VISITOR to a hotel in Scarborough was asked at breakfast how he would like his eggs cooked.

"I want one so hard that it would bounce, and the other so soft that I could drink it with a straw," he replied.

"I'm not sure we can manage that," said the waiter.

"Why not — you did it alreet yesterday."

OVERHEARD ON seeing the first snow of the year:
"Aye. I see yon hills have gitten their shawls on."

A BRIGHOUSE man wanted a divorce from his wife because she kept goats. The solicitor said there were no grounds for divorce because she kept goats.

"Oh, but she keeps them in t' bedroom and they smell."

"Couldn't you open the window?" the solicitor said.

"What," replied the man, "and let all my pigeons out? No fear."

A TYPICAL example of Yorkshire humour can be seen carved at the end of a pew in St Mary's Church at Sprotbrough near Rotherham. It is called 'Before and After Marriage'.'Before' shows two heads facing each other, whilst 'After' shows two heads looking in the opposite direction.

Said of a hard worker:
    "She'll go to heaven reight enough. I reckon they'll give her a job polishing wings."

A LAZY lad got a job working on a building site near Barnsley. He set off with his wheelbarrow upside-down. His boss looked at him and said:

"Get thi barrer reet way up".

"Nah," he said, "sumb'dy 'll put summat in it."

A MEAN old farmer near Thirsk had a new live-in labourer.

"Have some pudden, lad."

"Yes please, sir."

"What did tha say?"

"No thank you, sir."

"That's it, lad — thee speak up."

Overheard in a Baildon pub:

"Me throat's that dry, a pint'll nobbut wet one side."

A WEST Yorkshire teacher, conducting Bible study, came to the Beatitudes and said: "Blessed are they who mourn — what is it to mourn?"

A small boy said: "It's Sat'day".

"Look, dad — I've med Meg look nice for t' sheepdog trials tomorrow."

THE QUEUE at the Sheffield post office was getting longer and longer. At its head — in front of a grille labelled 'Pensions' — a little old lady was taking her time. She fumbled in her handbag, brought out first one and then another article, and laid them on the counter. They made an imposing collection. The pension book still hadn't come to light when a man further back, with a soldierly look about him, piped up:

"Hurry up now, ma. This is a pay parade not a kit inspection."

Commented a Skipton millworker:
"I doan't get a big wage but I work according."

A WESLEYAN chapel near Bradford carried a simple notice in big red letters. It just said: "Think."

A wag added two more words: "Or Thwim."

A NIDDERDALE farmer walked into his local garage and said:

"Wilter 'eve a good luk at yon tractor. It in't rattlin' reet this mornin'."

A SUNDAY school teacher at a Nonconformist chapel in Calderdale was telling her children about Moses.

"What do you know about Moses?" she asked.

"Ah knows 'im, miss," commented one child. "They put 'im in a basket and chucked him in t' river."

A FARMER in the former West Riding went to get his petrol coupons just after the war.

"I's gitten a tractor and a gelding," he said to the government scrutineer.

"What do you use them for?"

"Well I uses t' tractor for cartin' stuff rahnd farm an' fer tekking milk rahnd. I use t' gelding for scrattin' muck around."

"I see," said the scrutineer "Let's say twenty gallons for the tractor and fifteen gallons for the gelding."

The farmer went out clutching his coupons and with a broad grin on his face.

A SOUTH Yorkshire miner had a famous whippet which won many valuable races.

"Wot dost tha feed thi dog on?" he was asked.

"Beef steaks and mutton chops when I can afford 'em," was the reply.

"An' wot when tha cannot afford 'em?"

"Well, then it has to live t' same as us."

OVERHEARD IN a Leeds music hall:

"The art of magic is fast disappearing."

WHEN TIMES were hard in the 1930s, an out-of-work collier went for a walk with his dog. A passer-by said:

"Why don't you sell your dog and buy a pig. That way you wouldn't go hungry."

"An' wot a fool I'd look setting off to go rattin' wi' a pig."

"The trouble with you, Fred, is that you've got no ambition."

AN AMERICAN visitor to Yorkshire asked if there were many Chinese living in the county, as he had been to a rugby league match in Hunslet and overheard this little snippet of conversation:

"Well we wun yan."

"Dister, but how long sen?"

A NORTH York Moors farmer was describing an over-miserable lady:

"She teks mo-or pleasure at them she sees in t' church-yard nor what she hears in t' church."

A WAKEFIELD man was invited out by a posh friend who insisted that he drank wine with dinner rather than his usual pint of mild.

"Whativver is that i' me glass?" he asked.

"It's called claret — don't you like it?"

"Like it?" was the reply. "If it cost nowt it were too dear."

Instructions given to a Dales fire brigade in 1904:

"They shall make with all possible speed to the engine house; will take orders from the foreman; and when they are ready to start will take their appointed seats on the engine. On arriving at the fire they will dismount and stand by the side of the engine until the word of command is given by the foreman. It cannot be too strongly stressed on the engineers that they should avoid if possible spraying water on the bystanders."

A HARD-DRINKING Barnsley millworker was asked by a friend what he would have to drink.

"Thanks, lad. I'll just have a mouth full of mild."

"No tha wont. Tha'll just have one pint like the rest on us."

A BRADFORD woolworker was talking to his wife about friends who had died.

"Have you ever thought which of us might die first?" asked his wife.

"Aye, lass. I've said to mysen many a time that if owt happened to either of us I'd go to live in Skipton."

THE TASK of a parish clerk in a village near Beverley was not a full-time job by any means, and he described the sexton's work with a spade:

"Six full days and he could bury the whole of the parish."

ONE YORKSHIREMAN'S view of marriage:

"Nivver thee marry a woman wi' a fortune. My wife 'ed five pound and I's nivver heard the last on it."

A HAWES woman's opinion of her slow-going son:

"Oh aye, our John, 'e's just like a cow's tail — he's allus behind."

Overheard on a bus after a very poor summer:

"Where did you spend your summer holidays?"

"In my overcoat," was the reply.

A BILSDALE farmer's wife was raising turkeys, and on a cold December night all of her flock went missing. She went out with a torch but found no sign of them. She went out again early in the morning expecting to find a massive fox kill. Then from the branches of conifer trees all the birds came down to be fed. They had roosted all night well away from the crafty fox. Bird brain? Not likely.

In November 1942, wartime evacuee Nora Sanderson wrote:

"EVACUATION IS ringed with painful associations for many unfortunates but, far from being bored, I found my seventeen months in the Settle district a wonderful experience, and will try to write a few of the strands which I shall never forget and for which I give thanks.

"I delighted in the natural beauty, and a complete contrast to the fear and cruelty at this time. I am no Wordsworth but I think none of us who lived in this county, austere but tender, grand yet homely, without being the better for it.

"Always there was the wide and changing pattern but stable with the beauty of Ingleton and Penyghent, of hill and stone-walled moorland, where one could walk undisturbed except for the sheep scrambling over the tops. I see the steep little roads and walled green lawns, the narrow streets of upper Settle, the comely grey houses of Giggleswick, the ubiquitous green dome which one began by disliking but grew rather fond of.

"The other day I was in a large town which was busy with buses and cinemas, and shops as soulless as a slot machine; I was insecure and lonely, and all because the place was too big and gave no sense of rest. I thought of Settle, quiet under its hills. I thought of how lucky I had been to live in, and share in the doings, serious and frivolous, of a place small enough to be loveable and retain tranquility.

"Thank you, Settle! I felt very peculiar when I first arrived in your market place, but now I know you and your heart is warm."

The waller

A tanner a yard the wallers they earned,
Their monuments still stand for their trade was well learned.
For mile after mile over hill and through dale,
They can withstand the storm and the gale.

They sweated through summer and froze in the cold,
To earn a living their labour they sold.
Six days a week they would toil at their craft,
Until Sunday gave respite from their graft.

Strange terms and words these men they would use,
The batter, fillings, top-stones and throughs.
But now not many wallers have their skill to hire,
For farmers mend their walls with rolls of barbed-wire.

Ken Ranson

THE VICAR was examining the Sunday school's Bible knowledge.

"Who was the mother of Moses?" asked the vicar.

"Pharaoh's daughter," replied a bright young lad.

"No — that's not right. We know that Pharaoh's daughter found Moses in the river."

The little lad smiled and replied:

"Aye, but that's nobbut wot she said."

A HAWES clergyman was reading the Bible to an ill old daleswoman. When he came to the passage "There shall be a weeping and gnashing of teeth", he paused to let the full meaning of his words sink in.

"Ah" said the old lass, "let um gnash um as them as can. I've had none for more than thirty year."

A BARNSLEY miner saw a chap in a pub looking very upset.

"Cum on, lad," he sympathised "Wot's up wi' thee?"

"I'm just lonely," he replied.

"Eeh, lad, wot will thee 'ave to drink?"

"Ta, I'll have a double whisky."

The miner glared at him.

"No wonder tha's lonely," he said and walked away.

A WORKER in a woollen mill walked into a butcher's shop window, pointed to a sheep's head and said:

"I'll 'eve one of them overlookers."

"That's nut an overlooker, that's a sheep's head."

"I kna', that but it will be if tha teks its brains aht."

A COLLIER came home from work black as coal after his shift. This continued even after brand-new showers were installed. His wife noticed that he was mucky but his mate was as clean looking as a new pin.

"Dost tha kna' why my Ned's allus mucky when they've got wun o' them showers?" she asked his mate.

"He allus uses them," was the reply, "but he won't tek 'is cap off."

A POLICEMAN found a miner lying drunk. He nudged the chap and said:

"What's tha bin suppin?"

"Whisky."

"Were it neat?"

"Nah, tha daft bugger — it were in broad dayleet."

THE YORKSHIRE sense of humour is often seen at its best on and around the sports fields.

In a competitive cricket match near Scarborough a young batsman was hit on the head and taken off bleeding. He was a baker in the town and a voice from the crowd called out:

"Tha'll be reet, lad. If tha'd bin hit by one of they pies it would have killed thee."

JOE MERCER was playing for Manchester City against Sheffield Wednesday and the referee called him up for a rough foul.

"Nay, ref," said Joe, "what would thi do if I called thee a wazzock?"

"Come on, Joe — I'd have to send you off."

"Right, ref — what would thi do if I only thought you were a wazzock?"

"I can't stop you from thinking."

"Reet then — I think you are a wazzock."

Both fell into tucks of laughter and the game continued.

IN THE 1950s Eric Clay was one of the best rugby league referees. He had warned a Bradford Northern player several times about over robust tackles. As another came in, Eric called him over and said:

"Can you just nip off and ask if my bathwater is ready. There's only ten minutes to go. Don't bother to come back."

The player was still laughing as he walked off.

AT A keenly contested cricket match in South Yorkshire, where feelings ran pretty high and the umpires were of doubtful integrity, a batsman was given out on a very questionable decision of lbw.

The unfortunate batsman demonstrated at the wicket that he could not possibly be out and he then walked to the pavilion, protesting on the way.

As the batsman was nearing the pavilion and the commotion had subdued, a wag called out from the crowd:

"Thee look in t'paper toneet — tha'll know whether tha'r art or not."

THERE WAS a telephone call to a Yorkshire team in the lower reaches of the football league. The official answering was asked:

"What time's the kick off?"

"What time can you get here? If you fetch a mate tha'll double t'gate."

FOOTBALL MANAGERS always get the blame when a team is doing badly, and the following was overheard in a certain pub on a Friday night:

"T' manager's poorly,"

"Wot's up wi 'im?"

"He's in bed wi' a bad side."

IN A Doncaster pub a morose drinker was asked how his fancied horse in the 2.15 had gone on. He replied:

"It were alreet — it cum third in t' 4.30."

A MAIN feature of any Yorkshire farm, especially in the Dales, has to be concerned with the shepherd and his sheepdogs.

Only those who have tramped over the Pennine uplands and seen the shepherds and their dogs at work can have a true conception of sheep farming in the Dales. Swaledales and other fell breeds are both fast and heavy, and can traverse long distances across the unfenced moors. The modern walker may boast of some of his walking feats over the Three Peaks and other fells, but if the distances which some of the shepherds cover daily were added up we should find a far greater mileage has been accumulated at the end of the year.

The shepherd cannot choose his times for visiting the moors; when the sheep have to be tended he must go, wet weather or fine, snow, storm or sunshine.

It is only natural that such a land of shepherds and sheep should be the home of many of the most famous sheepdog trials throughout the land and, in normal years, the contests held at Kilnsey, Bingley and Harden and other parts of the Dales attract shepherds and collies not only from Yorkshire but all over the land.

Although a time limit is set for each competitor, it must not be thought that the shepherd and dog which complete the procedure in the shortest time are bound to win the contest. Points are given for driving, gathering, penning, pace, forcing power, firmness, coolness, steadiness and obedience, so that older and mature dogs often triumph over younger and speedier rivals.

A hill shepherd's life

Now! Close thine 'een my lile luve
T' wind is at rest on' thi sweet dove
I' t' wicker cage nae longer calls
To coosheds ay and boundary walls.

But noo, lile luve, its time for sleep
May Matthew, Mark, Luke and John keep
Thee safely here sae snug and warm,
Shelter thee from life's lambin' storm.

Dorothy Una Ratcliffe

A POSH-SPEAKING rambler accosted a Swaledale farmer over a fence.

"Does it never do anything but rain in this place?"

"Aye lad — stay till tomorrow. It's goin' to snow."

A PASSING hiker approached an angler on the Wharfe near Grassington.

"Is this a good river for fish?" she asked.

"It must be," the fisherman replied. "I can't get any of 'em to come out."

WHAT DO youthful visitors to the Dales find to put in their great rucksacks which need so much carrying? Some of our fell farmers went into the hills for the day carrying nothing but a raincoat and a packet of sandwiches. Their name for the small bag in which these were carried were called haversacks. This was derived from the small bags in which the old-time drovers carried their staple diet which was haver bread — a sort of oatcake. Hence we have the origin of haversacks.

ONE GARDENER to another:

"Some folks will pay the earth for garden compost. I gets mine from a mucky pile by yon wall."

A HOLMFIRTH resident's opinion of a new housing development in the area:

"A bungalow is a reet name for yon spot. T' job were bungled fra start to finish, an' t' chap it were built fer is still paying fer it."

AN OLD farmer told a visitor:

"When they say that winter's comin', I does not believe 'em. They said the same about summer but it nivver cum."

In the 1950s a dalesman described modern dancing as "a quiet country walk impeded by the opposite sex".

A SKIPTON farmer was once heard to say that he put in fifty stitches. By this he meant that he had put in fifty rows of potatoes.

"I know they say that a dog is a man's best friend —
but that's twice this week he's borrowed a fiver off me."

OVERHEARD IN Bradford market.

"What dosta think of grafitti?"

"I don't like any so-art o' foreign food," was the reply.

A dalesman told a girl that if she refused to marry him he would 'dee'. She still refused and he did 'dee' — but eighty-three years later.

AT HAYTIME on a farm near Settle, Old Bob who did not seem to be working very hard as he swung his scythe. He was singing:

"Milk and bread I nearly deed,
Milk and bread I nearly deed."

The farmer told his wife and that they had better do something. Next morning old Bob was working like a demon and still singing, but this time the words were changed:

"Bacon an' eggs teks care o' thi legs,
Bacon an' eggs teks care o' thi legs."

"DECEMBER 9TH 1944. An adventure with a cow today! We walked from Hellifield through Otterburn and along the Airton road to a barn where we had left the tractor. As we were filling it with not-too-clean water, using the leakiest bucket in the world, a farmer's man rushed round the corner shouting for help — so off we dashed to find a cow in a pit of liquid manure. The poor creature was out of its depth and in a sorry plight indeed. Fortunately our foreman was with us and between us we managed to hold the cow's head up, one girl clinging to its tail. Another ran to tell the farmer and get a rope. We heaved and tugged but hadn't sufficient strength between us to hold on to the rope until two farmers in their best breeches came tramping down the road, probably on their way to the auction. They quickly came to our aid and together we pulled the poor frightened creature out. There was such an odour that we nearly passed out on the spot."

Mary Sykes (Land Army girl)

In the classified ads section of a Dales newspaper:

"Lost, stolen or strayed — a steam - roller. Anyone finding the same will be rewarded."

A FARMER'S wife's diary for March 1952 recorded:

"Harry bought a new gallon milk-can and the price was 35 shillings. He says it will not stand up to heavy wear and tear, yet the one it is replacing is fifty years old and bears testimony to fine workmanship."

THERE WAS a man living near the River Nidd who decided to build a boat in his attic. He did a wonderful job, but the boat was so big that he could not get it out.

I remember, I remember

I remember, I remember,
Rag and bone men in the streets.
When he came round shouting "Rags and bones"
We were in for a special treat.

Yes, I remember very clearly
If a bag of rags you could fill
You'd get a little goldfish
Or a lovely coloured windmill.

Yes, I well remember
Other special treats.
Take your jam jars back to the Co-op
And you'd get a bag of sweets.

Then there was the lamp lighter
Around the streets he tramps.
He would come around each evening
Lighting all the lamps.

Where have all the Anderson shelters gone?
If my forgetfulness you will pardon,
Where have they all gone to?
There used to be one in every garden.

Woodbines were eight pence for twenty.
Three pence for a loaf of bread.
No one had heard of sliced bread,
They used a knife instead.

But there were children sweeping chimneys.
Scarlet fever and rickets ran rife.
Malnutrition there was in plenty.
For some, forty years was the expectation of life.

So as I sit and ponder
As back in the past I gaze,
And I ask myself this question
Were they really the good old days?

Monica Guiry

"I'm giving up going to church for Lent."

DURING A Sunday morning service in a small village church in Swaledale, the congregation was singing Fight the Good Fight when suddenly the strains of the organ (which was manually blown) died away with a squeak. A few brave souls tried to carry on singing but they soon gave up. Presently the door of the organ loft opened and a small tousled-haired lad peered out.

"T' feyt's ower," he said. "T' blowers broked."

OVERHEARD IN a Yorkshire mill:

"Our jobs are now in jeopardy."

"Well, I'm mun movin' theer — tha'll 'ave to sack me fust."

WHEN THE pig killer came to the farm, the farmer's wife said:

"You know I'm not a good farmer's wife. A good farmer's wife ends up in the cemetery."

The man thought for a while.

"Aye lass, tha's reet — and bad uns ends up thee-er an' all."

CLATTERING UP the cobbled streets at night, the dashing horses of the mail coach pulled up in the market place at Ripon. This was a gallant and exciting incident. And when you knew that the driver and the sorter were arriving, it stirred up in a youthful imagination desperate affrays with the Dick Turpins of the time. Letters arriving in such a spectacular fashion always seemed to be more precious.

Overheard in a Scarborough pub:

"Them there regrettas will be startin' any time nah."

A LITTLE girl, when she misbehaved, was put into the 'naughty room' and her collie dog obediently curled up with her. One day her grandfather was talking about a young lad who had been stealing his apples.

"E's a reet naughty un," said the old man.

The collie looked at him, went into the naughty room and fell fast asleep.

"I WAS born in Sheffield in September 1940, just a few months before 'the Blitz'. During my childhood, my grandparents used to stay with us from time to time and I was fascinated by some of the expressions my grandfather used to use. In particular, he used to say 'There's old in four-penny', which seemed to mean that people had hidden depths. For the life of me, I could not work out how this expression had come about. It would remain a mystery for many years.

"In years gone by, before the days of heated buildings and when winters were really cold, it was sometimes difficult to brew beers in midwinter. Some breweries use to brew extra beer during milder weather of such high strength that it could be stored for several months in the brewery cellars ready to be supplied into the trade as required. These old ales, as they were called, potent and matured to a mellow smoothness, became very popular and many breweries served them alongside their regular beers.

"Working men in those far-off days were reduced to drinking cheap, mild ale known as four-penny because the price charged was only four pence a quart. On occasions, when they could afford it, they would improve their drink by mixing half a pint of old ale with their half of four-penny. This is how I learned about the origin of my grandfather's expression and solved the riddle of 'There's old in four-penny'."

Frank Priestley

AT BAINBRIDGE in the upper valley of the River Ure a farmer blows the forest horn on winter evenings. Dalesfolk do not like a lot of frills to life, and the hornblower has no special clothes. They do insist on punctuality which is why he has never been able to listen to the nine o'clock news.

At Ripon-on-the-Skell, a tributary of the Ure, an even more famous horn is blown nightly, but this time throughout the year. The people of Ripon do like all the historical frills and they have decked their hornblower in a buff coat with scarlet cuffs and collar. The brass buttons have the corporation insignia featured in relief.

Bainbridge uses a horn from the African buffalo, though that is not the original horn which is preserved at Bolton Castle. There is talk of the custom going back to the days when a Roman fort stood in the village and it is certainly old enough to have been of value in the old forest days. It was a case of you would be able to 'hear' the horn from the wood.

Ripon has a similar horn and the original is treasured by the corporation. Ripon knows rather more about the history of hornblowing, which originated in the ninth century, when the chief citizen was the wakeman, who was responsible for the safety of the household goods and property of the Ripon people.

Hornblowing is a specialist occupation which tends to run in families, and somewhere along the line you discover an association with a Yorkshire brass band. It needs a well-developed pair of lungs and the ability to 'blow your own trumpet'.

A Dales thought

No Northern heart can ever lose
The proud affection felt for those
Great dales of Wharfe and Swale and Dent.
The hills of Whernside, Penyghent
And Ingleborough, Fountains Fell.
Of Kilnsey, Ribblehead, all tell
To those at home or exiled who
Enjoy the panoramic view.
Of pasture, moor and farm and fell
Which seem so silent yet can tell
Of life pursued in daily tasks.
Providing worthwhile fruits, and asks
That they and theirs may always find
Such quiet scene, and peace of mind.

F Allen

"It says: 'Get away from the rat race with our farmhouse holidays'."

AN OLD man was a hale and hearty old chap, who was advised to take more care of himself. He had walked six miles to his home without waiting for a train. He glared at his adviser and growled:

"Thee look after thissen, old lad. I'm nobbut ninety-two."

THERE IS no doubt that Dales farmers preferred to watch the sheep rather than relying on the weather forecast on the wireless. One shepherd called his flock of Dalesbreds a "bit of meteorological evidence knockin' abaht on four legs".

A SHEFFIELD steelworker was always complaining about the cost of living. He went into a local shop with an order for his wife.

"Ah wants a pound o' butter and a stone o' flour — 'ow much?"

"Let's see" replied the grocer, "flour is 2 and 10 a stone."

"Nah tha hod on a bit" said the steelworker. "Afore I'll pay all that, I'd eat dry bread."

From a rural almanac published in 1752:
"In December: keep your feet warm by exercise, your head cool through temperance, never eat till you are hungry nor drink but when Nature requires it."

A DALESMAN had an occasion to visit the vicarage and when he returned his wife wanted to know all about it. He told her of his experience in the big house and added:

"Tha knaws, lass, I think yon vicar's gittin a bit short-sighted."

"What meks tha think that?" asked his wife.

"Well, I wor nobbut in there fer ten minutes and he asked me three times 'Where's your cap?'"

"What about it?"

"Well, it were on mi 'ead all t' time."

A SWALEDALE-BASED sheepdog trainer was showing his farm to an American visitor. There was a request that he should put his dogs through their paces, so the trainer sent two of them up to the top of the fell to gather the sheep. The dogs went out of sight for a few minutes and returned with the sheep.

"That's swell," said the American, "but where are they going now?"

"Well, sometimes the sheep are in a hurry and knock down bits of t' wall," said the trainer with a twinkle in his eye. "They've just slipped back to wall up t' gaps."

In the 'Nature Notes' column of the April 1953 issue of Dalesman:

"Wild daffodils are out in the woods. The buds are awake but not yet dressed up."

A YOUNG farmer had had a little too much to drink one weekend, and on Monday morning he found himself in front of the magistrate.

"You've had a pint in the Red Lion at one o'clock," he was told by the magistrate, "and at two o'clock you had three pints at the White Swan."

"That's reet," admitted the lad."

"But where were you in the interim?"

"Nay, your honour, I've never bin i' that pub i' me life."

AFTER AN energetic dance at a Nidderdale 'social', a young farmer returned a pretty girl to her seat.

"Ee, lass," he said, "that were a good 'un. I's nivver sweat as much sin' I took my prize heifer to Pateley show."

IN 1953 a Nidderdale newspaper reported:

"If young, curly, four-inch-long bracken shoots are boiled in slightly salted water and served with butter, they taste like asparagus and made a very tasty dish."

There was a letter in the following week's edition:

"I have tried boiled bracken and cannot recommend it. The taste is very bitter."

"23RD DECEMBER 1944. Brilliant moonlight this morning. We all sat in the depot steps and greeted each new arrival with 'Good morning to you' sung at the top of our voices. Down to the farm for dinner where I accepted the farmer's wife's offer of meat and vegetables, a welcome change from the inevitable sandwiches of which we were all heartedly sick. In the stone sink was a colander full of hens' heads, which made me shudder, but it reminded me that it was Christmas.

"Back to Settle from Hellifield by milk lorry, a bumpy ride on the top of milk churns. A festive dinner at the hostel for which put on our best bibs and tuckers. The staff joined us to partake of roast beef and vegetables, Christmas pudding and trifle. Then a cigarette and three cheers for the staff. Delicious."

Mary Sykes (Land Army girl)

OF ALL the famous writers who have visited Yorkshire, none has left such a black mark on the fair shire as Charles Dickens. Bowes will always be associated with Dickens and Dotheboys Hall in *Nicholas Nickleby*. In Dickens' day, Bowes and its neighbouring county was well known for its many private schools, Dotheboys being one of several such schools.

The Unicorn Hotel, where Dickens stayed, is still flourishing. If you have the good luck to stay there, you can see the tiny room where Dickens is said to have written some of his words, and you may dream of him listening to the local gossip in the bar parlour before retiring to that cosy room at intervals to lash himself into a fury about the demon 'Mr Shaw' of Dotheboys Hall.

But the truth is even stranger than Dickens' fiction, and the fact is that Dickens only paid a furtive sort of visit to Dotheboys and only stayed in the village for a few hours, which speaks volumes for his powers of imagination but not much for his accuracy.

One only has to glance at Dickens' pseudo-Yorkshire accents to perceive how little relation to Yorkshire the story has; and the alleged Yorkshire characters are equally grotesque. This perhaps explains why Dickens was in such a hurry to leave Bowes.

There is, of course, no doubt that the private schools were not all they should be, but it is open to question whether 'the notorious Yorkshire schools' were worse than any others. As a matter of fact William Shaw, the supposed original of Wackford Squeers, was not a Yorkshireman but "a crafty and unprincipled London schemer".

THE HUMBER ferry chugged its way across to Lincolnshire. When the vessel reached the other side, a child's voice rang out from among the general chatter.

"Mummy," she asked, "is this America?"

A DALES farmer is a waste-not want-not man. He wants to use every bit of wool from his sheep. The shepherd stands with his legs apart and the sheep facing him is induced to pass through whilst he clutches the loose wool on the sheep's back, which comes off easily. The shepherd calls his bandy legs ''og oles'.

AN AMBITIOUS salesman knocked on the door of a remote cottage in the Three Peaks and asked the woman:

"Can I interest you in a set of encyclopaedias, madam? Your children will find them useful going to school."

"Nay," was the reply "They can walk theer an' back like I had to."

In the school history exam, one lad wrote:
"Sir Walter Rally circumcised the world with a big clipper."

SEVEN-YEAR-OLD Lucy was telling her granddad what she had learnt about the Second World War after the school trip to Eden Camp Modern History Museum near Thirsk:

"In wartime, children who lived in big cities had to be evaporated because it was safer."

THE INFANTS class was learning all about air travel, when one little girl piped up:

"Miss, helicopters must be cleverer than planes — not only can they fly through the air, they can also do the hoovering."

LONG GONE is the craze for chewing tobacco but it was once very common. Before that it was a common sight to see county folk chewing straw, locally called 'bent'. In Dent there was a saying

> *"Thee do as they does i' Dent;*
> *If thee has nah tobaccy, chew bent"*

ON THE subject of cheese, friends have quarrelled, families have been divided, and a vast total of words poured onto paper. I do not know whether any musicians have been inspired by the subject but poets certainly have. Professor Moorman once wrote:

> *"Oh, Swaledale's good for horses*
> *And Wensleydale for cheese*
> *And Airedale folk are as busy as a bee."*

Although this is pure Yorkshire, William Shakespeare wrote the wise words:

> *"I will make an end to my dinner,*
> *And there's pippins and cheese to come."*

Mr Kit Calvert of Hawes is not only a practical cheese-maker but also an authority of Wensleydale cheese. It has been recorded that it was introduced by the fore-runners of the monks of Jervaulx who originally came from Northern France and that it was originally made from ewes' milk. The tradition they created was left after the passing of the monks and has been maintained into our own times by farmers' wives in our northern dales.

Whether Wensleydale cheese is as good as it once was is one of the controversial issues upon which men fall out. There are those who remember the old farmhouse cheeses, blue, creamy and sweet without a trace of acidity, and who will tell you that the present-day product, though better than no Wensleydale at all, is but a pale shadow of the real thing. Others will tell you that this is but a legacy of wartime necessity and the real Wensleydale cheeses are on their way back.

THERE WAS a farmer in Dentdale whose great pleasure on Sunday was to visit one of the small chapels in the surrounding district and there 'expound the Word'.

He was so engaged on a particularly hot Sunday afternoon. Before the sermon was half finished, the elder end nodded their heads as they hovered on the verge of sleep. The children seized the opportunity and did almost everything that young lads should not do when they attend a place of worship.

With great difficulty the farmer continued talking to the nodding adults and whispering children. At last he could stand it no longer and, after a pause of several seconds, he exclaimed:

"Be quiet, lads, ye'll waken yer fathers."

AN OLD widow washerwoman in a Leeds suburb married a man a lot younger than herself. The vicar was surprised at her taking the plunge again and asked if she had given up washing clothes for a living.

"No I hasn't. I couldn't wheel it aht and peg it on t' line myself. So I'd had to choose between weddin' 'im or buying a donkey."

A WOLDS man was asked:

"Was your garden any good this year?"

"Aye," was the reply. "If it hadn't bin, folks next door would nivver have won first prize at t' annual show wi' their chickens."

Sign spotted in a baker's window:
"Cakes like your mother used to make, £2.50. Cakes like she thought she used to make, £5."

SOME VICARS are more popular than others. A church-warden visited a remote farm and was asked:

"What dusta want?"

"We're collecting fer t' church."

"Well I've nowt for thee. Wot's it fer anyroads?"

"It's a leaving present for t' vicar."

"That's different — thee wait then and I'll give thee summat."

I HAD always associated the craft of bespoke shoemaking with certain old-established firms centre on London's Mayfair and St James's. It was a surprise to find boots and shoes for individual customers still being made by hand in Grassington [in 1953], within sound of the River Wharfe.

Seventy-nine-year-old Arthur Inman is always seen in and around Grassington wearing a pair of his highly polished products. He is literally a walking advertisement.

Should Mr Inman agree to make a pair of shoes for you, you will fist stand shoeless on a clean page of a ledger which has been placed on the floor. The many previous pages bear the foot outlines of previous customers together with neatly written notes on subtleties and variations of those feet. From the 'foot picture' the lasts are made up methodically and moulded into the shapes of the left and right feet.

The shoes are made from the highest-quality leathers. Because of its supple qualities, 'willow calf' is best for the uppers, while 'oak bark' makes the soundest soles.

Arthur twines his own stitching thread from spools of bootmaker's fine white hemp. He waxes, twists and weaves the final thread, using to proof the thread his own mixing of pitch, resin and boiled oil.

It is no wonder that handmade shoes and boots are expensive, but they do last almost a lifetime if they are kept clean.

"By gum, Ah reckon if a ham sandwich costs that much, Ah've a pig that's worth £5,000."

GEESE MAKE good watchdogs, and they disturbed a farmer near Pickering in the middle of the night.

"Wot's up?" asked his wife.

"There's a fox after mi geese."

The farmer rushed out of his door, and two hours later he woke his wife who heard him shouting:

"Come on, lass — let us in."

He had run out in only his shirt and socks but the door had locked behind him.

"What's up with thee?" she shouted from the bed-room window, only to hear the plaintive reply:

"I's locked out and I'm nobbut starvin' to dee-ath."

"Say 'Moo'."

IN A village outside York, an aged resident was reproved for digging his rather large garden, and told that a rotary plough would complete the work in half an hour, and the cost would only be a few shillings. The octogenarian observed:

"So long as yan keeps clear of lumbagy, there's no exercise like diggin'; and when the day comes that I canna handle a spade, it'll be time for me to dig my own grave."

A Yorkshire farmer made a wooden leg for his wife at Christmas — and told her that it was stocking filler.

A TAILOR was delivering his wares in a Wensleydale village when her met a quarryman on his way home from work.

"It's a terrible thing," said the quarryman "that tha' nivver sees a tailor baht wot 'ee 'as a button off someweer."

"Aye," replied the tailor, "an' tha nivver sees a quarryman but what he 'as a few slates loose."

Overheard in the parlour of a family home near Huddersfield:

"Aye lad, tha can marry our Edna. But if I were thee I wouldn't tell her yet — she'd tell everybody."

AN ELDERLY man had been persuaded to attend a jumble sale in the Wakefield district, in aid of a local charity. He walked mournfully round the room several times, made a purchase and decided to go home.

"And what have you bought?" asked one of the organisers manning the door.

"Not mich," the old man replied. "Only one o' them Emmanuel saucepans for th' missis."

"IN OUR village there's this fellah what's known by 'is first name — and 'is last scandal."

A HOLDERNESS school was having an 'Animal Week' to encourage kindness to pets. One playtime a fight broke out between two boys, which was broken up by a teacher who asked how it had started.

"Well," replied one boy, "I kicked him for kicking my dog."

THEY HAD given a farmer a barometer to mark his silver wedding, and some days later he met an old crony who asked him if he liked his present.

"Nay," he said "Ah think nowt to it. You can't depend on it. One day it says one thing and t' next day it says summat different."

"Scalpel…"

OF ALL the Dales knitters, those at Dent have achieved the greatest fame. Theirs was no craft chosen as a light recreation; it was a hurried, nerve-straining rush to eke out sufficient money for a miserable existence.

The craft originated long before the eighteenth century when wool from the fell sheep was clipped, spun and knitted in the homes of the yeomen countryfolk or 'statesmen'. The products were carried on pack horses to Kendal market where they were sold.

Towards the end of the eighteenth century a new system was introduced, whereby coarsely spun wool, known as 'bump', was 'put out' from Kendal to be knitted by local farmers and their wives.

Each week, as the bump arrived at the house of the carrier, the knitters flocked round his door for their raw material. Shepherds on the fells, children at school and the women folk grouped around either doorstep or fireside, all were knitters. Each evening a different house was selected in order to conserve fuel, and in the dim glow they knitted with a peculiar swaying, bobbing movement known as 'striking the loop'.

Long after the bump knitting declined the dalesfolk of Dent continued their craft in the traditional manner, and knitting sticks and curved needles are still employed. Most of these are treasured relics of previous centuries made by fathers, grandfathers and villagers who were especially proficient at the task.

To a Craven gardener

I really cannot understand
Why you, who cultivate the land,
Should arrogantly pitch your tent
Beside the slopes of Penyghent.

For husbandry, however thorough,
Yields poor results on Ingleborough,
While horticulture was always a
Pursuit impossible at Feizor.

Then why so foolishly insist
On lighting bonfires in a mist:
And spend your leisure raising spuds
In intervals between the floods?

Those formidable limestone crags
Are only fit for hawks and stags,
And crops and flowers will not grow
Beneath so many feet of snow.

Even the greenest-fingered wizards
Are seldom at their best in blizzards,
You can't consider keeping bees,
They would inevitably freeze.

Abandon the unequal strife
With Austwick, just supporting life
Precariously, hand to mouth,
You'd do much better further South.

S D F

A WOLDS village was two miles from the nearest railway station and had only one bus a day. A farmer asked his neighbour who was going that way if he would ask if a parcel was waiting for him in the parcel office.

"Of course I will," said the neighbour.

In the evening when he returned, he just yelled out as he passed the farmer:

"Yes, it's there alreet."

A LADY, whose fair hair was darkening a little, decided that a special shampoo was called for. The next day her locks became a few shades lighter. During the evening meal, her teenage son kept giving her puzzled looks. After a while he asked:

"Have you been washing your hair?"

"Yes," she replied.

After another long silence, the boy said:

"By gum, it must've bin mucky."

AUNTY VERA had a golden labrador called Brandy, When her six-year-old nephew was asked in class about what he did on his Christmas holidays, he wrote:

"My grandma won on a horse and my Aunty Vera brought brandy and we played cards and had a party."

"OWER MAM has a new toaster," a small boy tells his friend. "It's reet clever. When t' toast is done, a bell rings."

"Ower mam's toaster's better," says his friend. When t' toast's ready, it sends out smoke signals."

AN OLD lady was visiting the Dales and spoke to an old shepherd:

"How wonderful it must be to live here; I suppose that you have been up and down these lonely fells many times."

The reply was "Nay I've nut, but me dog 'as."

"JANUARY 29TH 1945. There was great excitement when several of us were given bicycles to get to work. Some of us had never ridden one before. We went out in the half-light to the cycle shed and there were our cycles looking so new and smart. Although it was terribly cold and freezing hard, we were soon puffing and panting on our way to the Stainforth depot. The children of Stainforth — and there seemed to be hoards of them — made very sarcastic remarks as we passed by."

Mary Sykes (Land Army girl)

"Ah bet if we all 'ad a magic lamp each, t' Government would put a tax on genies."

TOM WAS engaged to a young lady. She had a twin sister who looked exactly like her. They dressed alike, looked alike, talked alike, acted alike.

A friend said to Tom:

"I should think you would find it very difficult to distinguish one from the other."

Tom replied: "I don't try to."

A JOINER went to a woodyard and asked for some 3x2 inch posts. The yardman said that everything was now metric and that the size he wanted was 7.5x5cm.

The joiner looked bewildered and asked how much it would cost. The yardman replied:

"Two bob a foot."

A BLUNT Yorkshireman was chairing a heated meeting of his board when the internationally respected finance director offered an unwelcome opinion.

"Shurrup," the businessman bellowed, "tha's only t' scorer."

WHEN YOU wander round old graveyards and read all these gushing tributes to the departed, do you ever wonder where they buried all the rotten people?

A CHEERY "Good morning, how are you today?" to the village roadsweeper produced a somewhat disgruntled reply.

"I'm fed up wi' this brush, I am. 'Ead's fallen off three times already this morning and now t' blessed 'andle's come out."

THE VILLAGE schoolmaster looked despairingly at little Janet's homework and sighed:

"I just don't know how one child can make so many mistakes."

The child replied helpfully:

"Oh it wasn't just me, sir. My dad helped too."

*"I don't know if you'll enjoy climbing Ingleborough tomorrow —
you'll break a leg tonight…"*

THIS TOOK took place on Market Street, Bradford. A
stranger asked an old-time tram driver to direct him to
Church Bank and received the following reply:

"Go straight on 'ear, nobbut ower thear, then rahnd
t' square at t' end, then tha'll see a church just aght o'
seet; turn left and yer'll be reight."

THE ORGANIST and choirmaster who served the West Riding church faithfully for well over twenty years was a real old Yorkshire character. He was a fine musician, although self-taught, and he spared no pains to see we had a very good choir.

When the choir was rehearsing Stainer's Crucifixion, the conductor made the members sing a difficult passage time and time again until he was satisfied it was near perfect.

"Nah then, lads," he said, "let's heve 'Fling wide the Gates' ower just once agean and think on, doan't hod 'em oppen sa long this time."

THE 'KING of the coil humpers' has been a serious competition where the winner has to carry a sack of coal weighing 110 pounds (50 kg) of coal on an uphill route of 1,000 metres — you see, even Tykes have gone metric.

This began when Yorkshire was a county full of coalmines, and Gawthorpe near Osset held the World Coal Carrying Championships. It is said to have originated in 1963 when two lads had a few to drink in the Beehive Inn. It was a case of "I'm fitter than thee and I'll race thee up yon 'ill we a sack o' coal on mi back."

There is a men and women's championship; the men's record is four minutes six seconds and the women's is five minutes five seconds.

There are strict rules. The sack is weighed at the start and then sewn up so that no coal can be spilled.

Even though the mines have closed the event still goes on, and the shout goes out at 12.30 —"Get humpin'."

A RIBBLESDALE farmer used to go to Settle market each week with his horse and cart. One day after his usual visit to the pub, and having had one over the eight, by the help of the landlord he got into the cart and set off for home. Soon he fell fast asleep. Some youths on the way saw how things were, unyoked the horse and let it go. Presently the farmer woke, took a puzzled look around and said:

"If it's me, Ah've lost an hoss; an' if it isn't, Ah've fun' a cart."

Passenger offering a £20 note to bus conductor:

"I'm sorry but I don't have any ten-pence pieces."

"Don't worry, madam, I can help you there. You'll soon have hundreds."

THE STORY is still told at Whitby of a holidaymaker who thought he would try his novice hand at fishing from the pier. He spent nearly an hour in patience before he reached up a very fine flatfish, which his fishing companions all envied. Then, suddenly, he threw it back into the sea.

"Why did you do that?" asked a fellow fisherman.

"Well, I don't want one that's been trodden on," said the holidaymaker.

TWO METHODIST ministers were being entertained to dinner by a local farmer. The farmer's wife had done them proud with two of their own reared chickens.

During the dinner, the farmer received an emergency call to his stock and, when he returned, the visiting parsons had eaten so heartily that they had cleared the lot and the farmer had to do with left-over corned beef. He felt a bit disgruntled but, after the meal, he took the preachers for a look round his poultry enterprise. The two men praised the excellency of his stock, especially his male bird.

"Aye," said the farmer, thinking of his missing out on a chicken dinner, "he ought to feel proud of hissen: he has two sons in t'ministry."

"It must be nearing his elevenses."

ON A lonely stretch of road in Swaledale a motorist ran out of petrol and, seeing a man with a horse and cart, begged a lift. A little further along the road the horse took fright and bolted, careering down a steep hill.

"I would give £500 to be out of this mess," said the city gentleman.

To which the Yorkshireman replied:

"Don't be rash wi' thee cash — tha'll be out for naught in a minute."

He was.

YOUNG SAM, a Yorkshire farmer's son, was staying with his American penpal's family. Members of the US forces, from the army camp nearby, organised a hay-ride to which young Sam was invited. The excited children climbed on to two huge army vehicles and, as they settled down, a very Yorkshire voice was heard to say:

"I thought we were going for a hay-ride — this is blooming oat straw."

TRAVELLING BY car through the Yorkshire Dales one summer, a tourist saw some beautiful old-fashioned flowers growing in a cottage garden. He stopped to look at them and then asked the elderly lady in the garden if he could buy a few. Without a word she went indoors for some scissors and cut almost half of them down for him and refused my money.

When he protested, she smiled and said:

"No thanks. It's the first time I remember having anything that anyone else ever wanted."

Yar Nelly

Yo' cannot tell yar Nelty owt,
Shoo knaaws it all, yar Nell.
Shoo wed gaumless gooid-for-nowt,
When shoo cud ha' had a swell.

Shoo's up at six, yar Nelly is,
Gets t'childer off ta t'schooil,
An' then shoo sallies aat ta biz
An' strakles lahke a fooil.

At whom, at neet, shoo fettles up,
Weshes, bakes, an' all,
At supper tahme fills t' kettle up,
Puts bottles raand us all.

Ah knaaw whoo's fifty pun i' t' bank,
An' means ta mak' it moor;
Sum fooalk think shoo's full o' swank,
Mesen Ah'm nooan so sewer.

Shoo says hersen it's nowt ta do
Wi' nubdy what shoo does;
Foaalk i' the'r juices han ta stew,
Shoo says hoo'l stew wi' us.

Yo' 'appen wonder ahr Ah knaaw
All this abaat yar Nell;
Ah'm t' gaumles gooid-for-nowt shoo saw
When shoo tonned daan her swell.

G A N

A MUKER man bought a very very second-hand car and proudly took a sceptical friend for a ride to display its good points. They laboured up hills and careered down dales. Then something passed them.

"What was that what whizzed by?" asked the proud car owner.

"Nay, Ah don't rightly know," said his pal, "but I think it were a traction engine."

THE WORD 'stot' means a bullock and this was transferred from the animals formerly used for draught purposes to the young men who dragged the plough round the village on Plough Monday — the Monday following the 6th January (Epiphany). It was on the Feast of the Epiphany that the men made their offerings of candles and other gifts at the altar of the church.

On Plough Monday they took out a plough and solicited offerings for their outlay in providing candles and gifts. They shouted and sang as they went on their rounds. Gradually a sort of rude pageant or play came into being. In time a 'Lord' and 'Lady' or 'Gentleman' and 'Lady' appeared at the head of the company, while collectors (known locally as 'Toms') and an old couple (T' Awd Man and T' Awd Woman) brought up the rear.

These teams have all but died out with the exception of Goathland and Sleights, and the last company has gone out in recent years. Our Goathland team have gone out regularly, with one exception in 1923. The war interrupted such activities, of course, but 1947 witnessed a bigger interest than ever.

JOHN AND Annie had engaged a labourer at Stockton 'hirings' to help on their farm, and were taking him home with them in their horse and trap.

Annie, who 'wore the trousers' in the household, was filling in the time (usefully to her way of thinking) by detailing to the man the various duties he would have to fulfil. After a three-quarters of an hour or thereabouts, she paused for breath, whereupon the new farmhand turned to John and enquired:

"Hey, mister, hast thoo much clay o' t' farm?"

"Nay, not si much, but mebbee there's a bit by t' beck i' t' Fower Yakker Field; it's clarty there. Why dost thoo ask, like?"

"Ee, that's a pity," replied the man, "Ah was aimin' ti mak thoo a few bricks i' ma spare tahme."

WHEN A venerable Wolds farmer was instructed by his doctor to have a simpler diet, he objected strongly.

"Aw'm nut gooing to starve mysen to death for t' sake o' living a few years longer."

A VEHICLE used a by-road in Wensleydale one Sunday. All the available car space inside was filled with wild flowers, foliage and even young trees. Uncertain of their route, they stopped by a farmer and inquired:

"Should we take this road back to Leeds?"

"You might as well," replied the farmer. "It looks as if you're taking everything else."

ERNIE WAS looking for somewhere to camp near Scarborough. A promising pitch was a nearby field and, seeing two small boys, he inquired whose field it was.

"Yon's Mosey's field," said the elder.

The little boy, aged about five, added dreamily: "Mosey's was the feller in t' Bible who saw t' bonnin' bush, and God said, 'Moses, tek yer beeuts off — yon's Holy Ground where yer stannin'.'"

A FARMER had been trying unsuccessfully for half an hour to get two mules into a horse box. The parson arrived just when the farmer's patience was exhausted.

"Now, Samuel. You look fairly bothered. What's the matter?" the reverend gentleman asked.

"Th' art just t' chap I wanted to see, parson," replied Sam. "Can ta tell me how Noah managed to get two o' these devils into t' ark?"

CHARLIE WAS desperate for work and had been all round the Cawood district without any success. The last straw came when he asked at a farm for a job making hay, only to be told by the farmer:

"The Sun makes my hay."

Next spring, labour was scarce and the boot was on the other foot. The same farmer approached Charlie and asked him to strike turnips for him.

"Nay," said Charlie, "the Sun makes your hay — then let the lightning strike thi turnips."

"Talking about religious views, vicar, I've got some lovely snapshots of York Minster."

Talk in the Buck Inn at Chop Gate was running on the wonders of plastic surgery. Old Fred Garbutt joined in.

"Oor vet's as good as onny on 'em," Old Fred said ruminatively. "Last harvest, t' lad chanced ti tek a greeat piece oot ov his thigh wi t' reaper.

"He was in a bad way, but t' vet come up tiv a new-cauven coo, an he fettled t' lad as weel — he just took a slice off t' coo's udder an' stitched it on, sharp as owt.

"T' lad mended quick, an' noo he's givin' three gallon a milk a day, sucklin' tweea calves, an' doin' a day's wark inti t' bargain."

A crusty old Whitby sailor, describing a persistent toothache:

"Well, it's in t' foremost grinder aloft on t' starboard side."

THE LADIES of the church sewing group were busy at their work, making kneelers, when in breezed the young curate.

"Well, ladies, have you thought what you're giving up for Lent yet?" he asked.

After the usual suggestions about giving up sugar in coffee or cutting down on cream cakes, there was a silence. Then one lady piped up:

"I've been thinking. I don't go to pubs or bingo and I don't smoke, but I do look forward to going to church — so I think I'll give that up."

A SMALL boy, in Grassington on a family holiday, asked a local youth if there was any fishing nearby.

"Aye lad," he was told, "there's a pond in t' wood."

"Thanks mister," the lad replied.

He rushed off, found the pond in question, giving but a glance at the sign which, had he been able to read, said quite clearly 'No Fishing'.

His concentration on angling was soon shattered when an irate voice roared in his ear:

"Carn't tha read what it say's on t' sign, lad — ner fishin'."

Taken aback, but quick as a flash, the boy replied:

"Don't thi believe it, mister — Ah've copped four already an' they arn't arf big uns."

FARMER'S SON, asked if he had liked his first day at primary school:

"No, and I'm not going back — it's all office work."

TWO PALS left Bridlington harbour in perfect weather and went out rather further than usual. They had been fishing for some time with great enjoyment when a sudden squall sprang up. The wind lashed the sea into great waves, the rain poured down, and their small boat looked in danger of capsizing. In great terror the two men began to pray aloud.

"Oh God, send down thy only son to save us," cried one, but his friend shouted him down:

"Nay God, cum down thisell t' save us, fer this is noa lad's job."

A LODGER in a London boarding house told a fellow resident that he had just spent a holiday in a Yorkshire moors village. He was asked how he had enjoyed it.

"Oh, it was a terrible place," he replied. "I think it was a waste of a holiday. You see, you couldn't get anywhere without walking."

Farmer to his wife, observing the work of the Electricity Generating Board:

"Look, them electric pythons are coming across our valley."

IT WAS at a revival meeting at a Dales chapel and the chapel was full to overflowing. Inside the building everyone was thoroughly warmed up by the singing and preaching. Earnest, pithy, Yorkshire sermons in the vernacular had been preached by those who had never preached before, and the fervour was growing apace.

Suddenly, the mother of a prodigal son cried out:

"Oh Lord, take ahr Jack an' 'od 'im by t' 'eels ower 'ell-fire woll 'is clogs drop off."

Then, thinking she had gone too far, she concluded:

"Ay, woll 'is clogs drop off — but nobbut give 'im a swither."

MILKMAN TO housewife on the day before a Bank Holiday:

"I was going to ask, love, if you'd mind me doubling up on you today."

GEORGE'S FAMILY holiday was cut short when he was called home, leaving his own family behind, due to his father being taken very ill and rushed into hospital. Accommodation for his invalid mother was secured in an old people's home, and for the next two and a half weeks he visited them both every day, fetched and carried, and generally ran about here, there and everywhere to please them. All without a word of thanks.

The day came for his father's discharge. George collected his father's clothes in accordance with his detailed instructions, and delivered them to his bedside, leaving him behind the bedside curtains to get dressed.

A moment later George was recalled. Secretly hoping he finally might be thanked for all his efforts, George inquired if everything was all right. He was told bluntly;

"Nay, lad, you've brought t' wrong tie."

WHEN JACK thought that visitors had stayed late enough, he would say to his wife:

"Let's gan to bed, mother; these folk'll want to be ganning hame."

THREE-YEAR-OLD SAM and his family were having a weekend break in London and were taking an open-top bus tour, with Sam pointing out places he knew as they passed.

"That's where the Great Fire of London started," he said, then, "That's Billingsgate Market"; and then, "That's the Tower of London where Paddington ate his marmalade sandwiches".

"It reminds me of the clouds round Whernside."

A company of senior citizens called the Evergreens were performing in a charity show at Whitby's Spa Theatre. After about forty minutes, the curtain came down for a scene change. Five minutes passed and there was still no cue from backstage to commence the next scene. Frantically, the stage manager tore backstage but, to his horror, he found no one there. Rushing upstairs to the dressing rooms, he saw the dear old ladies, all twenty-five of them, standing around drinking tea and eating sandwiches.

"What in the world do you think you're doing?" the stage manager demanded, almost lost for words.

"Well," said a young and sprightly seventy-year-old, "Charlie and 'is missus arrived wi' tea an' we thowt we'd sup it while it were 'ot."

WALTER MORRISON, MP for the Skipton Division, felt that he had been libelled by the Liberal newspaper the *West Yorkshire Pioneer*. He consulted his solicitor and election agent, Richard Wilson, and it was decided to bring an action in the High Court. When this was down for hearing in London, Mr Wilson, along with his witnesses, travelled to London and put up at the Inns of Court Hotel in Lincoln's Inn Fields.

On the evening before the trial, Mr Morrison provided a dinner at the Holborn Restaurant. After the loyal toast the guests were asked to drink "success to our cause". For these toasts, champagne had been provided. Later the waiter came round asking everyone what he would now like to drink. One guest, Jack Metcalfe, of Threshfield, replied:

"I'm not changing. That bubbly lemonade is good enough for me."

Next morning about six o'clock, Jack appeared at his bedroom door with sleeves rolled up and neck and chest bare, demanding of a startled chambermaid:

"Na lass, whar's t' kitchen?"

"Kitchen? It's downstairs; but what do you want with it?"

"Why to wesh myself. What's tha think?" replied Jack.

YOUNG CHARLIE was in church for the first time, and he took great interest in all that went on without saying a word, until the choir, all in white surplices, entered. Then he looked up at his mother in great excitement:

"Ooh look, mum, they're all off to get their hair cut."

"THE DALES are associated with some of the very happiest memories of my life.

"Oddly enough after I was demobilised from the army in the spring of 1919 the very first writing I was given was to do some articles on a little walking tour of the Dales, and I went, treading on air, a civilian again, a freelance journalist at last, through upper Wharfedale and then roaming about in Wensleydale. I shall never forget beginning that little walking tour.

"I have never found again — no, not even in the romantic islands of the West Indies, or in the South Seas, not in the deserts of Egypt or Arizona — the sunlight that set all the dewdrops glittering about my path that morning. And though many places have disappointed me when I have returned to them, the Dales have never disappointed me.

I still consider them the finest countryside in Britain, with their magnificent, clean and austere of hill and moor, their charming villages and remote white-washed farms, their astonishing variety of aspect and appeal, from the high gaunt rocks down to the twinkling rivers.

"As far as my present life is concerned the Dales have only two faults: they are not easy to get at from London, to which I am anchored for a good part of my year; and they have never offered me yet a country house suitable in size and type and cost to a family like mine. But I believe that one day I will return to their high hills and grey-green valleys and lovely peace. So please see that your new magazine fights to keep them all unspoilt."

J B Priestley, in the first issue of Dalesman *in 1939*